Kennywood

. . . Roller Coaster Capital of the World

Charles J. Jacques, Jr.

AMUSEMENT PARK JOURNAL

P.O. Box 478 • Jefferson, OH 44047-0478
(440) 576-6531 Fax: (440) 576-5850
E-mail: apjacqu@suite224.net

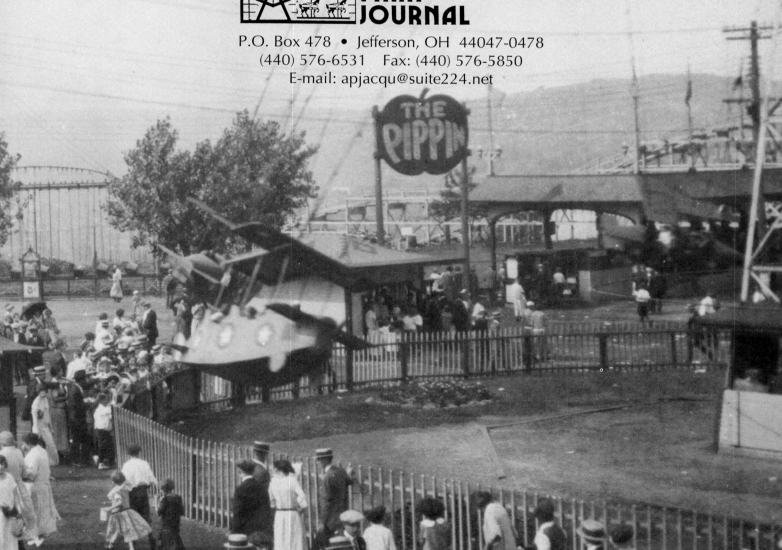

Contents

Dedication

To my wife Mary Jane
For encouraging first the idea and later the actual writing of the book.

Library of Congress Cataloging in Publication Data

Jacques, Charles J., 1940–
    Kennywood: the roller coaster capital of the
            world

    Includes index.
    1. Kennywood Park (Pa.)—History. I. Title.
GV1853.3.P42K464   790'.06'874886   82-2015
ISBN 0-9614392-5-4   AACR2

First printing 1982
Second printing 1988
Third printing 1990
Fourth printing 1994
Fifth printing 1997
Sixth printing 2001

Acknowledgements

The author expresses his sincere appreciation to the following persons without whose help this book could not have been written.

Carl E. Henninger, chairman of the board of Kennywood, opened the doors. He permitted the author to use the Park's correspondence which dated back to 1921. His family picture album from the early years was invaluable in illustrating the early 1900's. His first-hand accounts of the Park for 50 years answered many questions.

Carl O. Hughes, president of Kennywood Park, took an active interest in the writing of the book. He read the manuscript and encouraged the author. His help with historical interpretations was very important.

Harry W. Henninger, Junior, vice-president and general manager of the Park, shared his thoughts on the future of the Park as well as his recollections of the past.

F. W. (Bill) Henninger, president and manager of the Kennywood Refreshment Company, who like the other members of his family shared photographs, records, and love for the Park.

Andrew S. McSwigan, grandson of A. S. McSwigan and son of Brady McSwigan, who opened his files to the author. He also helped tell me more about his father's thoughts and feelings about the Park.

Andrew E. Vettel, the designer of the Thunderbolt and maintenance supervisor, gave "another" view of the Park—a view from the maintenance building and not just from the main office.

To Fred Weber and all the other maintenance personnel who have kept the Park running in good and bad years.

Ann Hughes, publicity director of Kennywood, made the Park's file of newspaper clippings available. She also helped the author use the Park's photographic archives.

Sylvia Kolar and Pauline Bendzock, Kennywood secretaries and picnic-bookers extraordinaire. They helped carry dusty packages of correspondence from the attic in the office so the author could use them. They also reorganized the files after the author had rummaged through them.

Below are just a few of the members of the "Kennywood family" who have spent years making the part what it is:

Susan Fontanese   Andrew R. Quinn
Kenneth Garrett   David H. Ruhe
Richard J. Henry   William J. Rodgers
Nancy Jane Jackson   Ray D. Waugaman
Thomas W. Lynch   Richard A. Wood
Edward J. McCague, Jr.   Alice Zych
Gary Paull

The Carnegie Library of Pittsburgh and the Pennsylvania Room of the library made their file of Kennywood Park available to the author. Also special thanks for the photographs from their photographic collection. The microfilm department of the library was helpful in filling in the missing years.

John Ross Thompson provided the editing and reading of the manuscript by a non-amusement parker. He made sure the public could understand complicated amusement park terms and concepts. Much of the punctuation and chapter titles are his work.

Joyce Diller typed the manuscript, helping turn scribble on yellow legal pads into sentences, paragraphs, and finally into chapters.

The author's father and mother, Charles Jacques, Sr., and Honora D. Jacques, who first took me to Kennywood when I was six.

The author's three children, Lynn, C. J., and Cory for reintroducing me to the wonders of Kennywood in the 1960's and 1970's. Cory deserves special recognition for one day asking me the question, "When are you really going to write that book?"

To the staff of Jacques and Jacques, P.C. including: Sharlene Bowman, Patricia L. Dutch, Barbara S. Gourley, Diane M. Mikolas, Linda R. Schaefers, and Linda Van Horn who have learned a lot about amusement parks over the last four years while helping me with the book.

Introduction—Labor Day

Kennywood Park illustrates the saying that the whole equals more than the sum of its parts, and this book gives a glimpse of the parts. Whether it is a roller coaster, merry-go-round, Noah's Ark, or Casino Restaurant, each contributes in a small way to the whole experience.

Other books have been written on amusement parks after they closed, Euclid Beach in Cleveland and Riverview in Chicago being two examples. All that remains are the memories. We are extremely fortunate that Kennywood can still be experienced in the whole from April to Labor Day—Kennywood can still be seen, heard, smelled, and even felt.

Kennywood Park cannot easily be put into words. Perhaps it best can be summed up by looking at the last day of the season.

Labor Day is always a bittersweet experience at Kennywood; sweet because it is the end of a long hard season of 16-hour days; the realization of a job well done with all of its highs and accomplishments. Bitter because there won't be any tomorrow, only a distant next season. Old friends will soon depart—many of them never to return again. The fun, excitement, and thrills will be gone and the ordinary everyday world will take over.

Labor Day starts at 11:00 a.m. when the earliest patrons come through the gate. The rides open and by noon it looks like there will be a good crowd.

Help in the Park is a little short because some employees had to return to school. Others must double up.

By the middle of the afternoon, the Park is in full swing. The stage shows are drawing large crowds, the stage act on the Island Stage is in full swing, and the roving bands and costumed characters are making their final rounds.

Many old friends and former employees come out the last day to say goodbye. Soon, twilight casts long shadows over the park. Lights come on, and it is time for dinner in the cafeteria or restaurant. The band organ plays its last few tunes, and soon it is closing time.

The park closes at midnight and within 30 minutes an eerie quiet has fallen over the park, broken only by the sound of the night watchman making his rounds. The park is closed for the season.

However, even on the coldest days of January and February when driving past Kennywood Park, there is a tingling, a certain feeling of excitement, a feeling deep down inside that Kennywood is only sleeping—waiting for just a little warmth and more sunlight to come alive again!

Poster from Trolley Car advertising, ca. 1929.

Trolley station, Kennywood Park, 1899, illustrating one of the disadvantages of Victorian-era skirts.

1

Kennywood—The Start of a Tradition

1898—the year America won the Spanish American War—was the year the Monongahela Street Railway Company leased a rustic picnic grove known as Kenny's Grove and 141 surrounding acres from Anthony Kenny.

The original tract of ground was purchased in 1818 by Charles K. Kenny, Anthony's grandfather, for five pounds, ten shillings, six pence and a barrel of whiskey. Together, Charles and his son Thomas, became rich mining coal from this land, sending it as far as New Orleans on flatboats they built themselves. Kenny's farmhouse was located on a bluff high above the Monongahela River. In the 1860's it became popular with local residents as a picnic spot.

Before the trolley line was built, picnickers reached Kenny's Grove either by horse and buggy on the Old Braddock Road or by steamer on the river which tied up at the coal docks. Kenny permitted people to use the local rustic grove of oaks and maples free of charge. Kenny's Grove was situated twelve miles from Pittsburgh, two miles from Homestead, and five miles from McKeesport.

At the turn of the century, trolley parks sprung up all over the Country. The Monongahela Street Railway Company decided in 1898 to build a trolley park at Kenny's Grove. Trolley Parks were a means of increasing ridership on the trolley lines. By offering rides, games, band concerts, food, and a picnic grove, the Trolley Company got workers and their

Anthony Kenny, the man who leased part of his farm to the Monongahela Street Railway Company in 1898.

Residence of A. H. Kenny, Kenny's Station, Mifflin Township, Allegheny County, Pennsylvania. Note the mine cars in the center background.

families to use the trolleys in the evenings and on weekends.

The Monongahela Line ran from Oakland through Squirrel Hill, past the steel mills of Homestead, and through the countryside around Kenny's Grove to the steel mills of Duquesne. This was the heavily industrialized Monongahela Valley which would provide the main market for Kennywood for many years.

The name Kennywood was chosen by the financially astute Andrew Mellon (a founder of the Mellon Bank and later secretary of the Treasury). Mellon, who held an interest in the Monongahela Street Railway Company, knew that Kenny's Grove was well known in the Monongahela Valley. Also, Kenny

had built up a lot of good will letting people use the grove free of charge, so Mellon secured the right to use the name Kenny in the Park's new name.

The Monongahela Street Railway Company used its own chief engineer, George S. Davidson, to lay out Kennywood and later he became its first manager.

Davidson's layout was practical and functional. The focal point of the Park was a man-made lake dotted with small islands and rustic bridges. Although only three feet deep, the lake still creates during the day and at night a beautiful mirror for the buildings and rides located around it. The original layout was so good that it has remained the basic design of the Park.

The Heart of Greater Pittsburg

Kennywood's open-air casino, operated by Franklin Wentzel from 1898 to 1945, who advertised "You Do Not Need to bring Picnic Baskets."

Peoples Popular Pleasure Park.

Gustav Dentzel of Philadelphia built Kennywood's first ride, a three-row menagerie carousel.

Kennywood's first major structures were all open air buildings: the Dance Pavilion, Casino, and merry-go-round building. They were placed at the ends of a triangle connected by wide gravel walkways. Davidson not only preserved the rustic beauty of the Park but he enhanced it by adding ornate gardens and hundreds of trees.

Kennywood Park had an historical spring of some note located where the Jack Rabbit is today. Here General Braddock stopped in July of 1775 with a force of 456 soldiers before approaching Fort Duquesne. General Braddock was killed and most of his troops massacred by the French and Indians in an ensuing battle. For many years this spring was advertised as an historical spot worth visiting at Kennywood Park. In the 1920's the Spring was filled in and forgotten, but in the 1960's an historical marker was placed on Kennywood Boulevard commemorating Braddock's Spring.

Most trolley parks were cheaply constructed, but all of Kennywood's buildings were substantial. The Casino and merry-go-round buildings are still in use and the dance hall was used until it burned in 1975.

When Kennywood opened to the public in 1899, a trip to the Park aboard an open air "summer" trolley was as exciting as anything the Park offered. The trolleys, which used their own right of way, had to climb a narrow winding route to reach Kennywood and the trip had several curves which seemed to be right on the edge of the cliff.

The trip to Kennywood offered a magnificent view of the Monongahela River Valley and the iron and steel mills at Braddock. At night the mills made a spectacular sight with the bright fires from their blast furnaces and coke batteries.

Kennywood's first ride was a beautiful handcarved, three-row merry-go-round by G. A. Dentzel of Philadelphia. This early Dentzel machine was a menagerie type with many types of animals and not just horses. All of the animals were stationary because a jumping mechanism hadn't been invented yet. There were winged chariots and a brass ring machine, and 16 large standing animals in the outside row. Twenty-seven years later, G. A. Dentzel's son, William, manufactured a magnificent four-row merry-go-round for Kennywood which is still in use today.

4

The dance pavilion was converted to a dark ride in 1953 after half-a-century of providing entertainment for patrons.

Lagoon and Bridge in Kennywood Park.

Boating scene as portrayed on a turn-of-the-century postcard.

Kennywood's first nationality picnic was for the Scottish Clans.

The open air Casino restaurant had a floor space of 72 feet by 120 feet with a surrounding promenade of 16 feet. Refreshment pavilions were placed in various places around the Park. There weren't any glass windows in the Casino until the 1940's; during the winter, the Casino was shuttered.

The dance pavilion on the far edge of the lake was a large wood frame building with exposed beams; it was two stories high with rows of screened windows around the second story. It was converted into a dark ride in 1953.

During the first season, free band concerts were offered in a small octagon-shaped building. These concerts proved so popular that the Monongahela Street Railway Company built a large, beautiful, new bandstand in the winter of 1899–1900. The octagon building was converted into a refreshment stand and, after many remodelings, it remains as the tower stand near the large restaurant.

Since the Railway Company paid a single charge for all the electricity their system used, they covered Kennywood with thousands of incandescent light bulbs. In 1899 when electricity was still a novelty to the average Pittsburgher, Kennywood Park at night seemed to be a magical fantasyland of lights and reflections.

Another attraction offered the first year was boating on the lake's water. At first the boats were made of wood but in later years they were of aluminum, and finally fiberglass paddle boats made their appearance.

Kennywood also offered tennis courts, croquet grounds, several games, a bowling alley, and a rifle range in a covered building.

The Trolley Company officials knew from the beginning that Kennywood could prosper only if it could attract picnics. The Park soon became the largest picnic park in Western Pennsylvania. Kennywood

Established in 1876 by John W. Black.   March Thirty-first 1900   Five Cents

PITTSBURG BULLETIN
A·WEEKLY·JOURNAL·FOR·THE·HOME

A NEW ATTRACTION AT KENNYWOOD PARK.—The Music Stand soon to be completed.—From the drawing by the designer, Mr. J. F. K....
This handsome stand will be placed in the northeast portion of Kennywood Park. The stage will measure 40x40 feet.

The new (1900) bandstand was previewed on the cover of the March 31st issue of the Pittsburg Bulletin. (Carnegie Library, Pittsburgh, PA)

was soon attracting schools, churches, and organizations for their annual picnics. The gathering of the Scottish Clans in 1899 was the first large nationality picnic to be held at Kennywood. It was soon followed by the Serbians, Russians, Slovaks, Carpathians, Irish, Hungarians, Polish, Croatians, and Italians—each with their own music, foods, dances, and languages.

For the 1900 season W. Larimer Mellon, nephew of Andrew Mellon and president of the Street Railway Company, had a bandstand built. It was one of the most beautiful buildings ever built at Kennywood Park. The bandstand cost $15,000 when a steak dinner with mushrooms cost 25 cents! It had a 40 x 40 foot stage with a beautiful proscenium arch 30 feet high. A white canvas curtain was hung from the arch for biograph pictures in the evening.

The bandshell had such perfect resonance that singers and speakers could be heard at great distances.

The boats in Kennywood's Old Mill surely have traveled millions of miles since it was constructed in 1901.

Even before amplification, the shell acted like a perfect "mike." The facade of the bandstand was covered with over 500 incandescent lights, and it had 3 dressing rooms on each side. The structure was used by numerous bands, choral groups and entertainers until it burned on opening day in 1961.

Also added for the 1900 season was a 400 x 400 foot athletic field. It had a covered grandstand seating 600 persons and two sets of bleachers, each seating 700. Many baseball games were held on this field until it was moved to make way for the swimming pool.

Kennywood's Old Mill was built in 1901. It had an old-fashioned mill wheel which propelled small boats through dark, dank tunnels. Flashing lights were used to illuminate grotesque and fantastic scenes. One of the first displays was Old Saint Nick emerging from the fires with a flock of his chosen elves. At the end of the ride the boats were pulled up a small incline and then sent down a small chute. The Old Mill was renamed and rethemed many times until it was almost completely rebuilt in the 1920's.

After three seasons, the Monongahela Street Railway Company had laid a good foundation for future growth. Kennywood was recognized as Pittsburgh's top park but times were changing. New thrill rides including scenic railways and figure-eight roller coasters were being developed and Kennywood was one of the first parks to build a figure-eight coaster for the 1902 season.

The Mill Chute was Kennywood's most exciting ride in 1901.

What with painted backdrops and dandy-looking employees, a trip to "Ye Old Mill" must have been a memorable experience. The promotional literature of the time referred to "Gorgeous Grottoes" and "Musical Caves."

Accommodations for large crowds of school children are such as to insure absolute satisfaction. Our facilities for handling large crowds will be better this year than ever before. Any number of special cars can be furnished to transport Schools and Churches from any point on the entire street railway system. Churches, Schools and Societies will have the privilege of collecting an admission fee at the gates if they so desire. The remarkable success of our concerts in the past has encouraged us to attempt greater things for the future, and some of the best organizations obtainable will be heard this season. The books are now open for dates for Schools, Churches, Organizations, etc.

Kennywood's management recognized early on that the Park's future lay in picnic business, to be secured through various churches, industries, schools, and community organizations.

2

The First Decade:
Kennywood Establishes Its Identity

Kennywood's first roller coaster was built by Fred Ingersoll, a Pittsburgh native.
Its new figure-eight design represented the latest state of the art in 1902.

TOBOGGAN

Three-Way Figure-Eight Toboggan. A most delightful form of entertainment for both old and young ◃ The strongest attraction ever offered Park Patrons ◃ ◃ ◃ ◃ ◃

This page featuring the Toboggan (which today we'd call a roller coaster) appeared in a 1902 promotional brochure "Pittsburg's Popular Parks," put out by the Pittsburgh Railways Company.

In the early 1900's Kennywood found itself in a fierce battle for patrons and picnics with thirteen trolley or railroad excursion parks in Southwestern Pennsylvania. The following parks drew the majority of their visitors from the Pittsburgh area: Oakwood (Crafton), Southern (Carrick), Luna (Oakland), West View, Dream City (Wilkinsburg), Coney Island (Neville Island), Rock Point (Ellwood City), Olympia (McKeesport), Aliquippa, Calhoun (Lincoln Place), National (Blawnox), Rock Springs (Chester, West Virginia), and Idlewild (Ligonier).

This was a period of corporate merger and consolidation, and trolley companies all over the United States were merging into large regional systems. Following this trend, Mellon's Monongahela Street Railway Company merged with several other trolley lines to form the Pittsburgh Railways Company.

Fred Ingersoll, a native Pittsburgher, designed and built Kennywood's first roller coaster, a figure eight, in 1902. He was a concessionaire for the coaster, which was the forerunner of today's Jack Rabbit, Racer, and Thunderbolt.

Pittsburgh Railways Company's promotional brochure for 1902 calls the figure-eight toboggan coaster

"the strongest attraction ever offered park patrons."

Here is how a writer for the *Pittsburgh Post* described a trip on the figure eight: "We went to a gravity railroad or whatever its name is—where you were hauled up an incline in a gaudy little car and then let loose, down, under, over, through, up around and back to the starting place at such a speed and by so many turnings doublings that you lost all sense of direction and all coherence of ideas."

This first figure-eight coaster was quickly followed by a scenic railway. The use of a chain lift on the figure-eight coaster and scenic railway permitted bigger dips and more speed.

These early roller coasters were different than today's coasters because they didn't have wheels under the track. They were held on course by side rails and when they hit a little rise they actually left the track.

A list of Kennywood's other attractions was included in a brochure *Pittsburg's Popular Parks* in 1902: rockery fountain, tennis court, row boats on the lake, shooting gallery, music stand, ample shelters, shady nooks, winding brooks, romantic walks, Ferris wheel, bowling alley, drinking fountains, pure air, rustic seats, figure-eight toboggan, cool retreats, green lawn, island dotted lake, photograph gallery, dining hall, athletic grounds, flowers, high class vaudeville, and shrubbery.

Even Andrew Mellon couldn't resist the lure of Kennywood. Years later Andrew Mellon's nephew, W. Larimer Mellon, recalled one fine summer night when he and his uncles went out to Kennywood Park "in summer flannels and straw hats. There Uncle Andrew, along with the rest of us, rode on all the rides and saw the vaudeville."

Because of the fierce competition, many trolley companies either closed their parks or sold them to new companies that only ran amusement parks.

The Pittsburgh Railways Company turned over operation of Kennywood to the Pittsburgh and Steeplechase Amusement Company. This company was incorporated to operate Kennywood and was headed by W. S. Dodge of Boston.

The Pittsburgh and Steeplechase Company introduced several new rides for the 1903 season: a Steeplechase Ride, a fun house, miniature steam train, and a Pony Track. The Steeplechase Ride was a small roller coaster with wooden horses instead of cars, racing side by side around a half mile track. The Steeplechase Ride was developed by George Tilyou of Coney Island, New York, but never proved to be popular at Kennywood. It was dismantled and removed after a few seasons.

Kennywood's first fun house was called "House of Trouble." It had a number of "innocent" amusements including a slippery slide, earthquake floor, and crazy stairs. In 1903 a three-story high circular slide called the "Dew Drop" or "Down and Out" was added to the back of the fun house whose name was changed to "Wonderland."

The miniature railroad had two steam-driven engines which went through the Wabash Tunnel to the "World's Fair." The Pony Track—located where Kennywood's office is today—had a number of horses and ponies. It also had several miniature curio ponies and was reported to have a herd of camels trained by "Arabs."

The
Great
Steeplechase
Horses
at Kennywood.

Greater Pittsburg's newest and most exhilarating amusement.

Everybody will be riding the horses this summer.

Half mile track.
Every heat is a race.
Beats every health tonic known.

The Steeplechase was introduced by the Pittsburg and Steeplechase Amusement Company for the 1903 season.

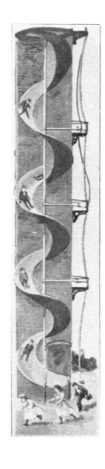

"Cast Up By The Sea," "California Red Bats," "Shocking Spring Water" and "The Dew Drop" were just a few of the attractions in the "House of Trouble."

The new Eastern Novelty, The Dew Drop—down and out.

12

Victorian styles had their hazardous aspects for these ladies attempting to negotiate the collapsing stairs.

In 1903 Kennywood ran afoul of Pennsylvania's Blue Laws which prohibited business on Sunday. Ministers from Homestead and Braddock went to the Park on Sunday to spot employees breaking the law. Later the ministers would return to Kennywood with constables to serve warrants on the violators.

To fool the ministers, employees wore a number of disguises. Nearly all wore green goggles and whiskers and mustaches made of curly hair. Some wore black faces and one of the barkers was cleverly disguised as a minister. Kennywood also hired employees who worked only on Sunday. It was argued by the management that employees couldn't be identified by the spotters. However, the Pittsburgh and Steeplechase Company was charged with 25 violations and found guilty in every case. It had to pay fines of $25 plus costs.

In February 1904, W. S. Dodge was ousted from his position with the Pittsburgh and Steeplechase Company, and he was replaced by the Moorheads of Sharpsburg.

The February 27, 1904 edition of *Braddock Illustrated* reported that Pittsburgh people took control of the Pittsburgh and Steeplechase Company and they

Harry and Gertrude Park performed their dangerous bicycle jumping act in front of the Fun House in 1905.

Official souvenir program for the "Great Western Train Hold-up" feature.

intended "To restore the Park to the state of respectability and popularity it was when controlled by the Mellon Brothers."

The first thing the new owners did was to rehire the head landscape gardener Mathew Ledward who had been fired by Dodge in 1903. Ledward was fired when his son wouldn't take on the extra job of oiling the Steeplechase Ride.

Hoping to improve attendance, the Moorheads brought to Kennywood a spectacular wild west show called "The Great Western Train Hold-Up." This production played for two seasons (1905 and 1906). It was given on the old athletic field which was converted into the Steeplechase Arena during the run of the production.

Thousands of feet of canvas were painted to look like the prairie with the Nevada Mountains in the background. This was then attached to the Scenic Railway coaster as the backdrop for the spectacular production.

At great expense a genuine Southern Pacific locomotive and several coaches were moved to the arena on the bluff from the Pennsylvania Railroad below. The cast included real cowboys and cowgirls and the leader of the outlaws, Scott Younger, had actually ridden with the Daltons and James Boys. A band of Sioux Indians camped at the Park for the summer. They played the role of allies of the outlaws. In the melodrama the outlaws held up the "Gold Express" at a small station, "Hole in the Wall" on the branch line of the Southern Pacific Railroad. Later they were caught by a group of vigilante cowboys and in the climactic scene several outlaws were hanged from a convenient telegraph pole.

Painted scenery on the framework of the scenic railway provided a backdrop for the western spectacular.

Rough hombres and prim Annie Oakley types shared the billing in the melodrama of the great western part of the United States.

Indians, outlaws, cowboys and cowgirls starred in the great western melodrama staged in Kennywood in 1905–06.

The Airship—a circle swing—featured gondolas of wicker. Note the bandshell in the background.

Here is how the wild west show was described in the show's souvenir program:

"In the presentation of 'the great western train holdup' the spectacular drama has soared to the loftiest heights of realism, and without equivocation this production epitomizes all that is grand, magnificent and inspiring in the idealistic representation of scenes in the far west."

The show also featured an exhibition of bronco busting and rifle shooting. The Moorheads found out that not only were the cowboys hard riders but hard drinkers. They had trouble keeping the show going all season.

But this spectacular production couldn't save the Pittsburgh and Steeplechase Company, which folded in 1905, returning operation of Kennywood to the Pittsburgh Railways Company. The Railways Company was forced to operate the Park for two years.

Although Kennywood didn't offer free acts on a regular basis during this period Park management did occasionally bring in a free attraction. One such attraction was Harry and Gertrude Park who drew a large crowd when they leaped a twenty foot gap on bicycles in 1905.

Operating the Park wasn't always easy, as could be seen in the report of two accidents in an issue of *Braddock Illustrated* published in 1906. It reported that a young lady was saved from drowning when she fell out of a boat into the three foot deep lagoon. Another accident occurred the same day when a car on one of the roller coasters broke through a guard rail with two girls narrowly escaping injury.

The Pittsburgh Railways Company was eager to get out of the park business and it finally found competent management when it assigned its lease with the Kenny family to A. S. McSwigan, F. W. Henninger, and A. F. Meghan in October of 1906. Operating under the name Kennywood Park Limited, these men were among the most knowledgeable park men in Western Pennsylvania.

Left: The new vaudeville theatre, in the Steeplechase arena, featured the latest European acts. Right: The famous "Life to Death" illusion was presented in the magic pavilion.

Andrew Stephen McSwigan had served for a number of years as the head of advertising and promotions for the Pittsburgh Railways Company. He was in charge of promoting the Railways' park (Kennywood, Southern, and Calhoun) as well as Duquesne Gardens.

Frederick W. Henninger was one of the owners of Conneaut Lake Park, and he had run games and concessions in a number of parks. He first became interested in the amusement park industry when he sold planking for early roller coasters. Henninger also had been one of the original organizers of West View Park in 1906.

Meghan had a reputation as the best picnic man in Western Pennsylvania. He had been manager of Kennywood under the Pittsburgh Railways Company and had been the first manager of West View.

The Henninger and McSwigan families have run Kennywood Park for the last 73 years. Probably the secret to their success was that they didn't wait for business to come to them but they went out and got business.

The McSwigan and Henninger families adopted a rather unique means of running the park. Although the park was a corporation, a member from each family starting with Andrew McSwigan and Frederick Henninger made day to day decisions while facing each other across a partner's desk. The main office of Kennywood was located in the Farmers Bank Building. During the summer, McSwigan and Henninger spent the afternoons and evenings at the Park.

Picnics became the backbone of Kennywood's business. While many other trolley and train excursion parks failed, Kennywood and West View managed to survive.

Small businesses in southwestern Pennsylvania were being replaced by large industries, so huge industrial picnics soon joined school, church, and nationality picnics at Kennywood.

The vaudeville season ran from early June to Labor Day. Acts like the Dumonti's Minstrels from the Eleventh Street Opera House, Philadelphia, appeared nightly at 8:15 sharp. In 1906 they burlesqued the wedding of Alice Roosevelt.

Before amplification live military bands played the popular music of the day. In 1907 the *Pittsburgh Leader* reported that "Nirella's Band will render selections afternoon and evening and added interest will be given the entertainments by the appearance of the well-known vocalist H. F. Blaney, who will sing the latest New York hits."

The new owners realized that roller coasters and thrill rides were needed in a proper balance with entertainment, food, and games, to sell picnics. They constantly updated, improved, and added new rides and attractions.

As the first decade of the Twentieth Century came to a close, Kennywood's new aggressive management was making plans for a sensational new ride—a racing coaster.

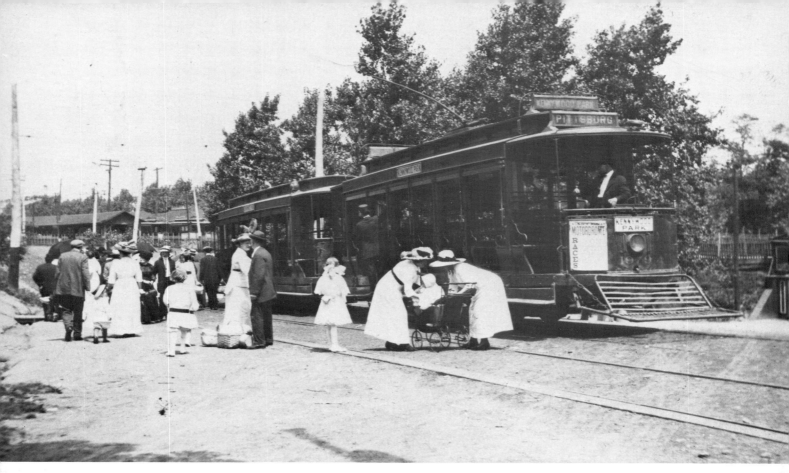

This open-air trolley, pulling a trailer, carried an ad for Kennywood's new Racer Coaster.

Coming out of the Old Mill in the early 1900's. The figure eight coaster can be seen in the background.

3

The Second Decade:
A Small Park Grows Up

This Racer Loading Station was located adjacent to the Dance Hall. The summer sun on this August day necessitated the use of umbrellas by the ladies, while the men wore their suits and hats in accordance with the styles of the day.

The Racer, originally called "The Aerial Racer—a Sensational Joy Ride," was built by the Ingersoll brothers in 1910. Costing nearly $50,000, the twin track racing coaster was the largest coaster of its kind in the world when built. The Ingersoll brothers had built Kennywood's first figure-eight coaster in 1902. The Racer had two trains racing side by side on two separate tracks but it still didn't have wheels under the track so dips and curves were gentle. The Racer was torn down in 1927 and replaced by Kiddieland.

Here is how the *Pittsburgh Post* reported the new coaster: "The new $50,000 aerial racer opened at Kennywood Park is proving to be the biggest sensation in the amusement world that has been offered Pittsburgh and Allegheny County residents for years. The great racing roller coaster or 'mountain joy ride,' the only one of the kind in the State, has proved itself more popular than anticipated by the wildest enthusiasts when it was opened for passengers. Thousands of people are flocking to the Park to get an opportunity to take this flying leap through the air."

Kennywood's scenic railway was replaced by a new coaster, the Speed-O-Plane, the following year. This new coaster, which cost $30,000, was built near the highway where pay-for-parking is today. The Speed-O-Plane was said to be "the longest and fastest ride in the country." The *Pittsburgh Post* commented that . . . "A. S. McSwigan has put it (the Speed-O-Plane) to a thorough test and had it in practical operation for nearly a week before opening it to the public. The ride is now pronounced perfect." Even the old figure-eight coaster, which was located by the main entrance where the Turnpike ride is today, was jazzed up with the name "Gee Whiz Dip the Dips."

Since Kennywood was developed as a trolley park, its electricity was direct or "trolley" current rather than alternating current. It was often cut off, leaving roller coaster riders halfway up the hill.

Many amusement parks in the early 1900's had unsavory reputations, as a number of them were controlled by people with low morals who permitted liquor and gambling. McSwigan's and Henninger's slogan was "no fakes, no liquor, no gambling and no disorder."

(Previous Page) This 1910 picture shows the new $50,000 "Aerial Racer." Note the Pennsylvania Railroad Yards and the Monongahela River in the background.

The loading station for the Speed-O-Plane. Kennywood's was built in 1911, and was one of the largest and fastest in the country. Note the side friction wheels.

A train starting out of the loading station of the Speed-O-Plane. Note the racer and airship in the background.

The first thrill of the Speed-O-Plane. Note the warning "Do not stand up" at the crest, and the tents used by picnickers on the ground at the left.

An aerial view of the Speed-O-Plane. Note the trolley on the old Braddock Road and the parking lot, still in an agricultural setting.

Electric lights were strung the length of the supporting cables of the airships, thus providing an exciting lighting effect at night.

Andrew McSwigan and Fred Henninger felt that amusement parks should be run in a clean moral manner. In 1920, they were instrumental in founding the National Amusement Park Association and McSwigan served as the first president. Now known as the International Association of Amusement Parks and Attractions, this organization continues to provide high ethical standards for the industry. McSwigan served as its president three times and other Kennywood personnel also have served as president.

McSwigan's and Henninger's policy for the Park was best shown by their 1915 slogan "anything not right will be made right." They knew that Kennywood's success depended on picnics. Picnics would come to Kennywood only if it provided a clean wholesome atmosphere. There was always a large disciplined police force, described like this in a 1914 brochure: "Courteous uniformed police are always present to suppress the slightest semblance of disorder."

High class vaudeville and magic shows were offered during the period. The old Steeplechase building was renamed the Hippodrome. Vaudeville featured six or seven acts with dancers, gymnasts, and ragtime singers being the most popular. The shows

Fun-seekers in their bowlers and hobble skirts on their way to the Daffy Dilla.

were held on Sunday afternoon. Joseph Nirella's Military Band, Vantine's Westinghouse Air Brake Band, and Danny Nirella's Band appeared yearly in the Bandshell and Dance Pavilion. The band concerts usually included the most recent hits and excerpts from new musical shows with a few classical numbers thrown in to round out the performance.

Kennywood also had a nickelodeon motion picture theater which burned in 1911. The fire was believed to have been set by burglars. The motion picture theater, penny arcade, and shooting gallery also were lost. A new larger building replaced the old theater, and today it is used as the penny arcade.

Motion pictures have appeared periodically at Kennywood. The first motion picture was Thomas Edison's "The Great Train Robbery," shown for the entire 1904 season. Motion pictures were shown again during the 1910's and talkies were presented in the 1930's.

Kennywood's publicity was by newspaper and poster. Pittsburgh had six major newspapers and there were dozens of small daily or weekly newspapers in outlying communities. Men called "snipers" were sent out to post signs on fences, walls, and telephone poles. The men were given $4 a day plus trolley carfare and bridge tolls.

Kennywood has always attracted people of all ages, from the youngest to the oldest, like the grandmother in the foreground.

Kennywood's first carousel was replaced by a $10,000 galloping model in 1913. It was built by T. M. Harton Company of Pittsburgh, the owners of West View Park. The new carousel was placed in the original merry-go-round building and a set of rings was added. In 1916, the Park also bought a new band organ from WurliTzer, and it is still in use in the Park.

Two other rides were popular in these early days at Kennywood. The Whip, built by W. F. Mangels of Coney Island, proved an instant success. It featured a speeded-up whiplike action as the cars make the corners of a rectangular track. It proved to be so popular that a Whip has been in the Park's ride list to this day.

The Circle Swing Airship had small ships made out of wicker, and this was one of the few rides not owned by Kennywood. It was owned by a concessionaire who paid rent to the Park.

Picnickers in a sylvan setting.

(Below) Lake Kennywood has always been a focal point for the park, and renting boats has always been a profitable business.

In the early days of Kennywood there were several footbridges crossing ravines. Today these ravines have been filled, and no footbridges exist.

Like the boats on the lake, this pony track is one of the Park's oldest attractions. For years the track was operated as a concession by Mr. McTighe.

The Old Mill, as well as were Kennywood's other major buildings, was outlined with numerous electric lights at a time when electricity was still almost a novelty for many patrons.

Young girls and ladies, all outfitted in white, await their turn for one of the park's Roller Coasters.

More games were added to the Park's arsenal and they played an important part in the Park. The games included: cane rack, rolling game, race derby, red devil, china kitchen, Silk Hat Harry, doll rack, and War Game. There were novelty stands, pool tables, and a bowling alley.

Even though roads in Western Pennsylvania were narrow, unpaved, and winding, more and more picnickers "took a drive" to Kennywood. So many came that the large lot across the trolley line was converted into a free parking lot. Free auto parking space was first advertised in 1916.

(Right) A nattily-dressed Policeman and a small crowd gather in front of the Daffy Dilla.

A Pool Room and a Bowling Alley were connected to the Daffy Dilla., A quick method of exiting the Daffy Dilla was via the slide in front of the Pool Room.

28

Picnickers watching the latest dance steps taking place in the open-air Dance Pavilion.

Kennywood didn't have its own railroad station until 1926. Travelers who came by the B&O, P&LE or the Pennsylvania Railroad had to get off at Rankin, Duquesne, or Braddock and take an open air trolley to the Park. In 1918 it only cost seven cents during the day or ten cents at night to go to Kennywood from Pittsburgh.

The fun house's name underwent the following changes—Wonderland, then Daffy Dilla Fun Factory in 1910, and finally Hilarity Hall in 1915. One of the major attractions in the fun house was a human roulette wheel. People would sit on the wheel and, as it gained speed, people would tumble off with only the person who was in the very center at the wheel remaining. Daffy Dilla was said to have "57 varieties of amusement where one can have more fun than can be furnished by a barrel of monkeys."

In the early 1900's, Kennywood offered a free children's playground. The playground had see-saws,

(Opposite) Concerts in the Bandshell have been a tradition at Kennywood for 70 years. The work of the musicians and entertainers was punctuated by the screams of patrons of The Racer in the back of the seating area.

slides, and swings. The pony track remained popular with the children.

Another new exciting amusement, a tilt house, was added in 1915. This ride was a small wood room or house which could be tilted on a large swing axis. Although people thought they were moving, they remained stationary and only the house moved. This illusion lasted into the 1920's.

The Old Mill was rethemed and renamed the Panama Canal in 1911, but after three seasons it became the Old Mill again.

In 1917 Andrew McSwigan wrote another amusement park owner, "Cleanliness is our motto and the World knows just what a job we have in our location fighting ore, dust and smoke from the surrounding mills. Incidentally, we're hoping for plenty of smoke this summer. The more dirt we have dumped on us, the more money we take in."

A fine aerial view of the Carousel Building and the beautiful surrounding gardens.

The Dance Pavilion was refurbished by McSwigan and Henninger with a beautiful floral ceiling. More lights were added. Dancing was carefully regulated and couples who wouldn't follow the rules were asked to leave. Dancing was offered every afternoon and evening with novelty dances on Fridays and Saturdays.

The restaurant, which was managed by Franklin Wentzel in partnership with the Park management, offered everything from a cup of coffee and a five cent sandwich to a ten-course meal. However, most people brought picnic lunches and ate in the two large covered pavilions which are still in use in the Park.

The Park even had its own barber shop in the service building. A visitor could have his hair cut in between roller coaster rides!

This period of growth ended when the United States entered World War I. For several months there was serious debate whether amusement parks should remain open during the War. Some picnics were cancelled, but Kennywood remained open during the War.

Andrew McSwigan answered amusement park critics in a letter to the editor in the *Pittsburgh Press*, February 12, 1918. "In strenuous war times outdoor recreation is needed more than ever before, especially in the industrial centers. The English government learned this after it closed and reopened the amusement places at the outbreak of the war."

The biggest picnic of the decade at Kennywood took place May 30, 1919, with the joint picnic of Carnegie-Illinois Steel and the Duquesne community. Franklin Wentzel employed 350 people to feed 30,000 people. Twelve thousand pounds of meat along with a roasting 1,000-pound ox were served. Coffee was served in two 500-gallon tanks which were heated by a huge fire of railroad ties. It was fitting that this decade of rapid growth for Kennywood should near its end with such an extravaganza. No more could Kennywood be called a small-time Park.

Crowds were large during World War I, to take in new attractions like the Tilt House which can be seen between the Racer and the Airships.

The midway, featuring the new ride sensation "The Whip" installed during the 1910's. Note the wording on the facade of the Shooting Gallery suggesting that men learn and prepare now for World War I military duty.

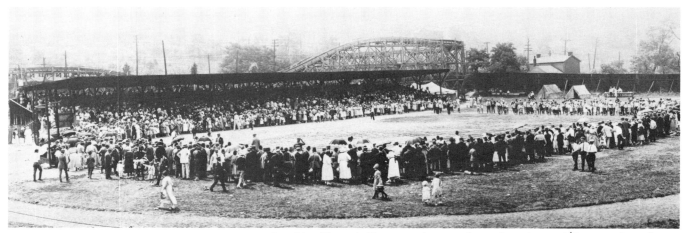

A foot race at a community picnic, on the old athletic field. Note the Speed-O-Plane beyond the grandstand.

Girls race at the 1916 Westinghouse Picnic. (The Carnegie Library of Pittsburgh)

Spectators, dressed in their finery, witnessing an athletic event on a field overlooking the Speed-O-Plane.

Above: Kennywood's management has always been conscious of the attractiveness of landscaping features, such as this small pool, rock fountain, and gazebo.

Center: A rustic arbor, adjacent to the carousel.

Below: Members of the office staff pose for this photographer in a nicely landscaped setting.

Above: In Kennywood's pre-Polaroid days, the photo studio was able to provide patrons with "Your photo in 10 minutes." Notice the cleanliness of the grounds.

Left: Mom and Dad and all their friends enjoy a days' outing.

4

The Twenties:
A Golden Age

The 1920's were a decade of speed, speed, and more speed. Lindbergh flew the Atlantic and radio went from a toy to a major method of communication and entertainment. Dance bands using radio developed regional and national reputations. Sound was added to the movies, making them even tougher competition for parks.

Kennywood not only adjusted to these changes, but was able to use them to its advantage. Additional rides, continuing Park improvements, and program specials made this a golden age for Kennywood.

There was a change in management when Andrew S. McSwigan, Kennywood's president, died unexpectedly January 12, 1923. His place was taken by his 32-year-old son, Andrew Brady McSwigan. Frederick Henninger, who was twelve years older than Brady McSwigan, remained as secretary-treasurer and became the senior partner. Brady McSwigan and Fred Henninger worked well together, both in making major decisions and in daily operation of the Park. Through their leadership, Kennywood continued to grow during the decade.

In the 1920's a group of park officials often met to eat a picnic dinner together on a patio in back of the service building. This group became known as the "Hungry Club" and included Frank L. Danahey, vice president; A. J. Wyant, manager; Robert W. Comstock, assistant manager; John Chapple, superintendent; John F. McTighe, manager of Novelty and Gift Stores; A. A. McTighe, manager of Theaters, Ponies, and Arcade; A. F. Kam, director of publicity.

(Previous page) The Jack Rabbit was Kennywood's first high-speed ravine roller coaster, where the dips took advantage of the natural terrain. John Miller designed this famous double-dip coaster in 1920.

From the lake, the Jack Rabbit appears to dip below the surface of the water. Note the large number of boats available for rent.

Andrew S. McSwigan was Kennywood's president from 1906 to his death in 1923. He was also active in newspaper circles, amusement park professional groups and fraternal organizations.

With its array of lights on the upper curves, the Jack Rabbit was especially appealing to ride at night.

F. W. Henninger was secretary-treasurer of Kennywood from 1906 to his death in 1950. He was the real finance watchdog through good times and bad.

In 1920 Andrew McSwigan and Fred Henninger hired one of America's top coaster firms, Miller and Baker, to design a new high speed coaster. John A. Miller designed the new $50,000 coaster. Taking advantage of the ravine in which the historic Braddock Spring was located, Miller designed the Jack Rabbit. Using a small amount of lumber, he designed a beautiful coaster with the new system of wheels under the track to create an 85-foot double dip.

The *Pittsburgh Dispatch* said that the new Jack Rabbit was attracting thousands of patrons to Kennywood. "Sensational dips, gigantic leaps, dizzy climbs make the new amusement the most popular attraction between New York and Chicago. A double dip and a long covered passage, in addition to the 85-foot drop, make it a real thriller."

In 1924, John A. Miller, who had formed his own firm in Homewood, Illinois, was hired again to design another coaster. This time he used the ravine at the opposite end of the Park in back of the Bandshell. The Pippin, which cost $60,000, also had a double dip.

The Racer, which was originally built in 1910, was showing its age by 1926. Plans were made to rebuild it, but at the last minute it was decided to demolish it and build a completely new coaster.

Left: The old racer, built in 1910, was razed in 1926. Kennywood's Kiddieland now occupies this area.

Below: Construction picture of John Miller's new racer, opened in 1927. Note how Miller built the return hill over and around the loading station.

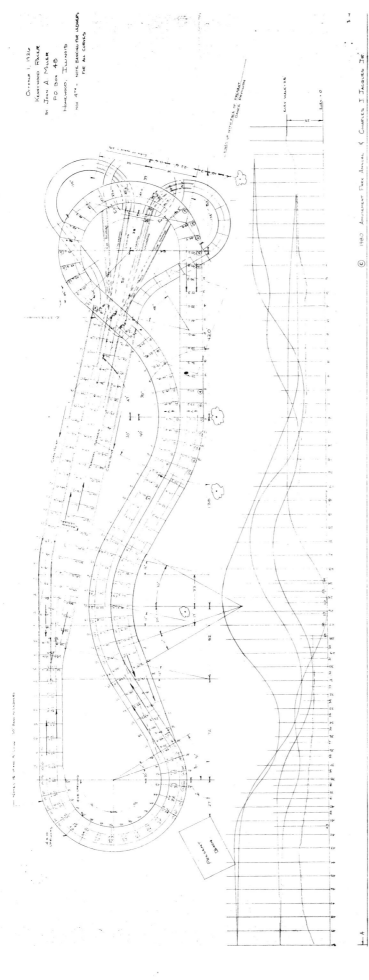

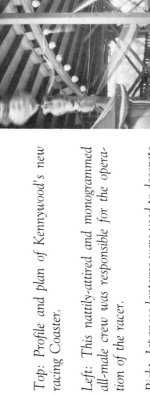

Top: *Profile and plan of Kennywood's new racing Coaster.*

Left: *This nattily-attired and monogrammed all-male crew was responsible for the operation of the racer.*

Right: *Japanese lanterns were used to decorate the racer's loading station during the Park's annual carnival week.*

The Pippin, completed in 1924, was the third high-speed roller coaster built by Kennywood Park, all designed by John Miller. It was the predecessor of the present-day Thunderbolt, which incorporated part of the ravine section of the Pippin in its superstructure.

Left: Harry Traver's Deluxe Seaplane replaced the old airships in 1926. In the background is the Pippin Coaster and the Bandshell.

Below: An aerial view of the Park, showing the new Dodgem, the Caterpillar, the Miniature Railway, the Seaplane, and the Swimming Pool, as well as the Jack Rabbit and the Pippin. Photograph ca. 1926.

Above: The midway, near the main entrance, showing the new Dodgem, The Old Mill, and the Vaudeville/Penny Arcade Building.

Below: Flappers and their swains admire the antics of the 22 Dodgem cars.

Because they liked John Miller's previous work, they hired him to build a new twin or racing coaster. Brady McSwigan wanted a "snappy ride that wasn't too much for mothers and children to ride."

The new Racer was one of the most beautiful racing coasters ever built. It cost more than $75,000 because Miller didn't use the topography as he had with the Jack Rabbit and Pippin. The highest hill of the new Racer was actually built in a ravine and much more lumber was required. Miller designed a reverse curve so that the train that started on the right side of the loading platform would finish on the left side. The new Racer had wheels under the tracks which permitted banked curves as well as curves on the dips.

Charles Mach, Kennywood's chief mechanic for over 20 years, supervised the on-site construction of all three coasters. His first job had been as a carpenter on the construction of Kennywood's first figure-eight coaster in 1902.

Upper Left: Taking advantage of the Tutankhamen craze, management re-themed their Old Fun House into "Tut's Tomb."
Upper Right: The park built a new bridge over the lake in the 1920's.
Below: Kennywood got dual use from this building, which housed a Penny Arcade together with the Vaudeville Theatre.

Other rides were added to meet the public's desire for thrills and speed. A green-striped, canvas-covered Caterpillar by Harry G. Traver of Beaver Falls was added in 1923. It was a circular ride with the cars riding an undulating track. The Caterpillar had a large fan under the track and management feared that the ride might be too risqué by blowing young ladies' dresses up, but this didn't happen and the ride proved to be very popular.

In the winter of 1921–1922, the old figure-eight coaster (which had been remodeled and rebuilt several times) was finally torn down to make way for the Dodgem. Miller and Baker designed the Dodgem building and fifteen cars were purchased. The ride

cost fifteen cents and was described as follows: "Dodgem runs like some people drive a Ford. One expects to go forward and goes to the rear. He steers to the right but goes to the left or whirls about."

The Dodgem paid for itself the first year of operation. In 1925, new, smaller and faster Dodgem Junior cars replaced old, slow Dodgem cars. A new 16-car Whip replaced the 12-car model in 1927. A Tumble Bug by Harry Traver was purchased the same year. Kennywood's first Tilt-A-Whirl was added in 1928 and placed next to the Racer.

Old favorites like the Fun House and Old Mill were redesigned to take advantage of the Tutankhamen craze. The Bug House became Tut's Tomb.

Above, Left: *The Tumble Bug, another ride by Harry Traver, was purchased in 1927.*
Above, Right: *A "country" theme was used in decorating the Old Mill for carnival week in 1927.*

Below: *The Bandshell remained the center of musical activity in the 1920's. Note the electrical American Flag added in the 1910's to the top of the structure.*

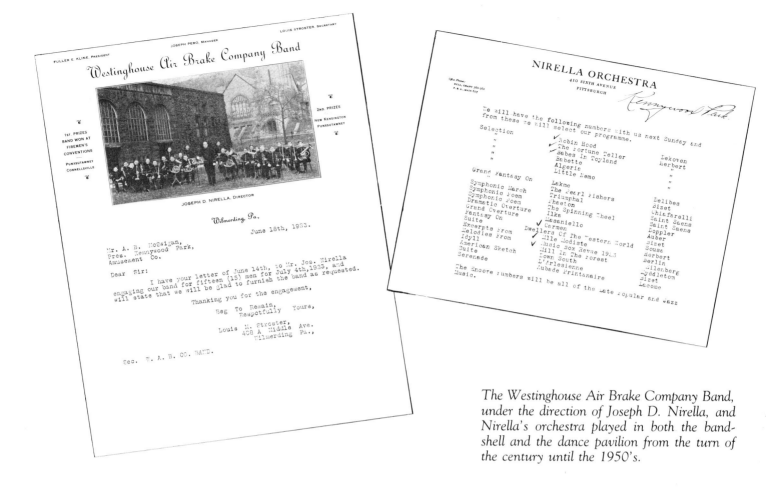

The Westinghouse Air Brake Company Band, under the direction of Joseph D. Nirella, and Nirella's orchestra played in both the bandshell and the dance pavilion from the turn of the century until the 1950's.

New stunts were added. A searchlight having a 21-inch lens whose light could be seen for miles was placed on the top of the Fun House. The novelty of Tut's Tomb wore off after only two seasons and the Fun House became the Bug House again. It had "57 varieties of rib tickling devices" such as human roulette wheel, barrel of fun, witching waves, revolving tub, laughing mirrors, and slide.

The Old Mill was completely reconstructed in 1926. The channel was lengthened to accommodate 25 boats and the old wooden structure was replaced by one of sheet iron. Charles Mach supervised the alterations. To make sure the channel dropped slightly its whole length, he rolled a bowling ball into the tunnel before it was flooded. Everyone waited with baited breath. Finally, the ball rolled out of the exit to cheers from the construction crew.

The Windmill, which looks like one of the oldest structures in Kennywood, was actually built in 1929. Brady McSwigan liked a windmill at Coney Island, Cincinnati, Ohio, and he had Charles Mach design it from a photograph. It was built on an island in the lagoon, and in 1939 it was moved to where it now stands by the Main Entrance.

August 15 to Labor Day had always been a slow period for Kennywood. To increase interest during this period, McSwigan and Henninger initiated a Mardi Gras Week.

Scattered throughout the Park in conspicuous places were cards reading:

CHEERIO!	
To Frown	To Laugh
65	Only
Muscles	13 Muscles
Must Work	Are Used
SAVE YOUR FACE	

The entire Park was decorated with bunting and banners in a carnival theme and confetti and serpentine paper were distributed. Fun seekers came in costumes such as Barney Google, Maggie and Jiggs, Dutch Cleanser Girl, and the Gold Dust Twins. In 1923 a Reo phaeton automobile valued at $1,775 was given away. Other prizes included two free trips to Atlantic City, Kodak cameras, and even a pair of men's shoes.

Lynch Brothers of New Haven, Connecticut were the architects for the new swimming pool facility, as shown in this rendering of their design.

By 1925, the two free trips to Atlantic City weren't necessary as the *Pittsburgh Sunday Post* said that "Kennywood Park management has moved a section of Atlantic City within two car checks of downtown Pittsburgh." Kennywood built one of the largest (350 feet by 180 feet) and most modern swimming pools anywhere. The pool, which cost $150,000 held 2,250,000 gallons of water. It had a colonial style pavilion with a 2,500-seat grandstand built over the dressing room. A 25-foot wide sand beach containing 20 railroad carloads of white sand surrounded the pool on three sides.

Beach guards were instructed to rigidly enforce prohibitions against one-piece suits, jostling and rowdyism, and diving from the rails. The women's dressing rooms contained electric hair dryers and curlers. It cost fifty cents to use the pool and an additional twenty-five cents to rent one of Kennywood's 4,500 sterilized bathing suits. Spectator tickets were ten cents each and children's tickets were twenty-five cents with suit rental fifteen cents.

Free swimming lessons were offered by Kennywood and the *Pittsburgh Press* in the large Kennywood pool

46

during 1928–1929. Swimming and diving were permitted but hugging and kissing weren't. In 1927 a Kennywood police officer warned a young couple to stop hugging and kissing or they would have to leave. The boy said he didn't see anything wrong with their behavior and they wouldn't stop. The policemen and beach guards separated them, escorted them to their respective bathhouses, and they were evicted from the Park.

In 1922, Andrew McSwigan even had to warn A. A. McTighe, Penny Arcade Operator, about postcards of a suggestive nature which were being sold in Kennywood's arcade. He wrote, "You must agree 'French Pastels,' 'Surf Queens,' and 'Water Nymphs' are not fit to place in the hands of school children."

But Kennywood was proud of the number of dolls given away by McTighe in 1923. "If placed eight abreast and six feet apart (parade formation) they will form a column twelve miles long," Andrew McSwigan bragged.

Free Sunday band concerts continued to be offered. In 1923, old favorite Joseph Nirella and his Westinghouse Air Brake Band bought new uniforms and new instruments costing more than $2,000. One popular Joseph Nirella number was a musical interpretation of the "Death of Custer." Other local bands were: T. J. Vatine's Westinghouse Band, Izzy Cervone's Legion Band, Art Giles and his Everglade

Above, Left: A colonial-style grandstand which seated 2,500 was built over the dressing rooms.
Above, Right: The Pool—bottom and deck, were completed early in the Spring when snow was still on the ground. Kennywood management didn't realize when they built the Pool that they would have difficulty in future years with mine subsidence.
Below: This construction crew stopped long enough to pose for this picture.

Above: Kennywood's Pool featured floating "Horses" for extra fun while frolicking in the water.
Below: No need for a trip to Atlantic City with Kennywood's 350 x 180 foot swimming pool! When built, it was the largest swimming pool in the Pittsburgh area. The $150,000 pool floated thousands of patrons with its 2,250,000 gallons of water.
Opposite: The aerial view shows the raft island and the diving tower. Notice in the back the Pippin Coaster and how it dips into the ravine.

Above: Kennywood's lifeguard with his monogrammed uniform poses with a few friends on the sand beach which surrounded the pool.

Below: Kennywood's Annual Baby Pageant to pick Pittsburgh's perfect baby, was held at the swimming pool.

In the 1920's the Dance Pavilion did more business than ever, what with the popularity of such new stops as the Black Bottom, Tut's Strut, The Lindy Hop, etc.

Orchestra, and Danny Nirella's Band which traditionally performed on opening day.

Daddy Long Legs Geiger and his Orchestra appeared the entire 1923 season. The band members were publicized as masters of syncopation who played music for the fox trot, the one step, and the latest rage, Tut's Strut.

More picnics were held every year. Most of them featured athletic contests including a tug of war, baseball game, fatman's race (over 200 pounds), women's race, and children's races. Motion pictures were taken at picnics as early as 1920 and were shown to picnic groups in the off season.

Starting in 1918, *The Sun Telegraph* held a special day for Veterans from World War I, the Civil War, and heroes of 1898. Disabled veterans were transported to the Park and were given free tickets, and donuts and coffee called "sinkers and java." Red Cross nurses had a special booth.

Lt. Jim Murray and Lt. Jim Vey, both of whom were pilots during World War I, piloted a forty-foot army captive balloon at Kennywood in 1922. It cost fifty cents to ascend 500 feet and $1 to go 1,000 feet. The four-passenger balloon proved a real advertisement for the Park because it was visible for miles.

Above: *The Dance Pavilion was remodeled with a Florida motif, in the 1920's. It remained an open building until the very early 1930's, when the advent of electrical amplification no longer required the walls to be open for the sound to attract those outside.*

Below: *Izzy Cervone's Legion Band made many appearances in the Band Pavilion during the 1920's.*

Above: One of the major Pittsburgh newspapers, The Post, advertised at the Park in the mid-1920's. Many newspapers in Western Pennsylvania held special days at Kennywood for their subscribers.

Below: Trolleys were a major means of reaching Kennywood Park through the 1920's.

Kennywood's first Kiddieland consisted of four kiddie rides, and was located across from the Jack Rabbit.

Small children got a park within a Park when four miniature rides were purchased in 1924 and placed in a fenced-in area near the Jack Rabbit. The first rides were small versions of Mangel's Whip, a two-row carousel, Ferris wheel, and swan swing.

When the Racer was demolished in 1927, Kiddieland was moved and four additional miniature rides—aeroplane ride, circular auto ride, small Brownie roller coaster, and boat ride were added. All eight rides could be ridden for twenty-five cents. The original two-row kiddie carousel was replaced by a three-row model. Kennywood continued to operate a free playground with see-saws, slides, swings, and sandboxes.

Brady McSwigan conducted a Kiddie's Day in 1924. Free tickets used only on the Special Kiddie's Day were distributed through a motion picture chain. Kennywood also provided the motion picture theaters with a film about Kennywood which they could use as a trailer.

For both young patrons and the young in heart, a new full-sized four-row carousel was purchased from William H. Dentzel of Germantown. It had been built originally for the Philadelphia Sesqui-Centennial of 1926. Dentzel missed the deadline and it was completed with only two weeks to go in the exhibition. He sold it to Kennywood for $25,000. Although he was seriously ill, and died early in 1928, Dentzel left his sick bed to supervise the installation in a new $10,000 steel frame building.

The carousel turntable was 54 feet in diameter. It had 50 jumping horses, one lion, one tiger, and 14 stationary horses along with four bench seats, all of which was lighted by 1,400 fifty-watt mazda lamps.

The old merry-go-round was traded in and its building was converted into a snack stand. Stools were placed at a soda fountain which featured Reick's

A Mangels Kiddie Ferris Wheel was one of the original four rides purchased for Kiddieland.

Little Elves provided the motive power in this Mangels "Brownie" Roller Coaster. This ride was added to Kiddieland in 1927.

The Kiddieland was located to the spot formerly occupied by the Racer Roller Coaster. In the foreground is a miniature version of Mangels' famous Whip, the Kiddiewhip.

Ice Cream. Chicken (springers) and waffle dinners with all the trimmings for $1.50 were the specialty of the Casino Restaurant.

After many years with no Ferris wheel, Kennywood bought a large one in 1927. Built by the Parker Company of Leavenworth, Kansas, the wheel had a lot of flash with 100 electric lights in a star design. It offered a great view of the Monongahela River Valley.

A Dayton Fun House electric railroad with two trains was put into operation in 1925. The small trains had headlights, foot brakes, and a sand bucket. The sand was used for traction on wet days. The railroad, which replaced the Pony Track, is located where the office is today and was a third rail system. It had a small tunnel which was used as a shed to store the trains, a loading station, a bridge, and warning signals.

In a pamphlet prepared for a Shriner's outing in 1921, motorists were told all roads leading to Kennywood were par excellent. "From Pittsburgh go out Bigelow Boulevard to Schenley Park. Through the Park to Murray Avenue and then follow the

A Miniature Railroad built by the Dayton Fun House was added in 1925. This train was operated by a third-rail electrical system. Note that the locomotive is patterned after its full size brothers of the era.

56

A new 16-car Whip was purchased from W. F. Mangels of Coney Island, New York and placed in a modern all-steel building. After a 15-year absence, the Park added a Ferris Wheel in 1927. It was a deluxe Park model with ten enclosed cars, and was supplied by the C. W. Parker Company of Leavenworth, Kansas.

The "Voice of Kennywood" studio was added in 1929, in the second story of a new Refreshment Building located near the Restaurant. It featured the most modern microphone and amplification equipment available at the time.

street car tracks to Kennywood." Patrons were advised to watch for speed traps at West Homestead and Duquesne.

Kennywood first started using its well-known yellow arrows on the highways in 1925. It purchased 200 left and 200 right arrows.

Kennywood Park Corporation even operated a service station in the free parking area across the road during the 1920's. Brady McSwigan said it didn't make much money but when a motorist needed services it made "friends for life."

To compete with radio, McSwigan and Henninger introduced the Voice of Kennywood in 1929. They constructed a new tower refreshment stand with a "radio" studio on the second floor. Edgar A. Sprague was the first Voice of Kennywood. He made announcements and played music through six large speakers located at spectacle stage, bandstand, swimming pool, old mill promenade, dance pavilion, and the tower stand. The system was so good that management bragged that "it could be heard in any part of the Park."

Free circus acts were first presented in 1927. The Island Stage was constructed in 1928 and enlarged to 50 feet by 35 feet in 1929. Some of the famous acts which appeared during the twenties were: Bill Ritchie, high diving daredevil and his diving nymphs; Cel Dora, who rode a motorcycle at speeds up to 60 mph in a large globe; John Robinson's elephants; and Mlle Therira and her royal puppet show.

A railroad platform was built along the Pennsylvania Railroad track in 1926 to accommodate a train of twelve coaches, and a steel shelter was added in 1928. Park attendants would meet each incoming

The Voice of Kennywood Refreshment Tower had a number of Graybar amplification units, located behind the grillwork.

train and check picnic baskets. They would carry them on a cart to the picnic pavilion.

Brady McSwigan had a weekly tabloid-size newspaper with eight pages, *Kennywood Illustrated News*, printed in 1928 and 1929. "Rosey" Roswell (later Pittsburgh Pirate broadcaster) was the editor of this in-house publication. It had a circulation of over 100,000 and was distributed by Boy Scouts from Pittsburgh and nearby towns.

Kennywood Illustrated News was used as a means of publicizing free stage acts, dance and concert bands, along with recent improvements. One feature the first year it was printed was a children's essay contest on "What I like best at Kennywood Park." First prize was ten dollars worth of amusement tickets. For adults *Kennywood Illustrated News* had a song-writing contest with a first prize of fifty dollars. Danny Nirella, Izzy Cervone and Charles Caputo were the judges on the best song about Kennywood.

Rosey Roswell knew how to get the reader's attention when he put pictures of bathing beauties in every issue to publicize Kennywood's huge pool.

One article in 1928's *Kennywood Illustrated News* contained a list of lost articles from Kennywood's lost and found department. Here are a few: ladies' old shoe, table cloth and silverware, black twin baby carriage, basket with over-ripe bananas, and green lumber jacket with initials A. B. McS.

The Park built this new building for its four-row William Dentzel Carousel. It was one of the last carousels built by Dentzel, and was acquired in 1927. It has 50 jumping horses, one lion, one tiger, and 14 stationary horses.

IF YOU DON'T KNOW—HERE'S HOW TO GET TO KENNYWOOD

To get to Kennywood by trolley from downtown, take Kennywood car on Sixth Avenue, Liberty or Fifth Avenues. There are two lines —Kennywood trippers, which come down Sixth Avenue, Liberty and up Fifth Avenue, and the Pittsburgh, Homestead, Kennywood and McKeesport cars—No. 68—which come down Fifth Avenue to Smithfield and up Sixth Avenue. The first named route is the best because on it are operated large double truck cars. Both lines run out Forbes Street and receive transfers at Forbes and Brady, Atwood Street and Forbes and Craig.

If you come from East Liberty, Penn Avenue, Butler Street, or Herron Hill sections, you can take any car on Center or Penn Avenues to East Liberty and transfer at Penn and Highland or Penn and Center to Kennywood via Shady Avenue cars. These cars will begin running about 11 o'clock.

If you have an auto or a Ford and are coming from downtown, go out the Bigelow Boulevard to Schenley Park and then to Murray Avenue. Or, you can go via Fifth Avenue to Wilkins Avenue and then to Murray Avenue. When you reach Murray follow the car tracks all the way to the park. Look out for the one-way sign at the end of the Homestead Bridge. Driving off the bridge turn to the right with the trolley tracks. If you live on the South Side and have a car, try the new McKeesport Boulevard from the end of Carson Street to Homestead. This is the new boulevard which was opened last spring. With the exception of eight or ten city blocks at the upper end of the South Side, the road is fine all the way to Homestead. Beyond Homestead the road is paved and while a little uneven, is safe on the top of Kennywood hill.

At the Park there is parking space for 2,500 or more cars. There will be no confusion about auto parking and no one need have any fears about not getting a place either in the Park or the large free parking space adjoining.

Special note to drivers—The City of Duquesne and the Borough of West Homestead are working overtime on the 15-mile-an-hour limit rule. Don't take a chance on the motorcycle cops spoiling a perfect day.

Top: Robinson's elephants appeared in the late 1920's and early 30's, on the island stage in Lake Kennywood.

Center: Spectacular circus acts were presented on the island before the bridge and stage were constructed. In this picture the band and performers had to take rowboats to get there. The band had to crown to fit on the tiny island!

Left: After the island's stage and speaker system were constructed, large animal acts were held on it. The best seats in the house were always rowboats.

60

Everyone seemed to own a car (or a Ford, as Kennywood ads put it) in the 1920's. Fortunately, the Park leased acreage on the other side of the road which had room for thousands of them. For a time, the Park even owned its own gasoline station. Note the third rail track for the Miniature Railroad, at the left.

Kennywood's Restaurant Stand in the early '20's sold a drink known as Phez, made from pure loganberry juice, and which cost 10¢.

(Prior Page) Kennywood was the first Amusement Park to give away an airplane. It awarded the small Waco biplane on Labor Day of 1928.

Music was the order of the day as one of the local bands played at the Restaurant Casino, thus providing pleasant sounds both for those eating and those passing by.

1929 was such a big year that the Park decided to give away not one, but two cars, —in this case, a Chrysler and a Plymouth. Many picnics had their own special stickers; the one below is from the Knights of Malta Picnic in 1927.

Kennywood Illustrated News was full of jokes and sayings like "If ignorance is bliss, what's the use of going to school?" It also reported that, at the annual employees' banquet, President McSwigan and Johnny McTighe introduced a new dance step to the female employees.

Many publicity stunts were held in the 1920's. A baby pageant was held with the winner being sent to Asbury Park, New Jersey. A bobbed hair contest and a perfect foot, ankle, and limb contest were held. In 1928, Kennywood was the first amusement park to give away an airplane. A Waco airplane was shown in the center of the park. Management proclaimed that the plane would attain a speed of 100 mph and it was a lot safer than any other make of aircraft.

Business was good in 1929 and McSwigan and Henninger topped it off with a spectacular carnival week August 26–31. It featured three star circus acts, fireworks, and nightly Mardi Gras dancing to Whitey Kaufman and his famous Victor Recording Orchestra. Two automobiles, a Chrysler four-door sedan worth $1,265 and a Plymouth Coupe worth $755, were given away.

In many ways this final Carnival Week of the 1920's was the Fat Tuesday before the Great Depression. In the 1930's Kennywood employees would often think back fondly to the "good old days of 1929," Kennywood's Golden Age.

Kennywood's employees had their formal portrait taken in 1929 on the island stage. This was the peak of Park employment until sometime in the 1950's. Even the visiting elephants got into the picture, but they had to stand in the back.

The 3rd rail electric Miniature Railroad was located between the parking lot and the Casino. Early in the 1930's it was moved next to Kiddieland.

With the construction of the new Swimming Pool in the mid-1920's, the Athletic Field and Grandstand were moved across the road and trolley tracks.

5

1930–1934:
Kennywood Survives

By the 1930's, the Midway by the Main Entrance had under gone a radical change. The Dodgem had been replaced by a Laff-In-The-Dark, a new front had been put on the Old Mill, and a giant Penny had been placed on the Penny Arcade.

The Depression was more than a period of slow growth for Kennywood; it was an all-out fight for survival. Parks were folding or going into receivership all over the Country. Used amusement rides were a glut on the market and manufacturers almost ceased new construction.

While Kennywood's business was off only 8% in 1930, the downward trend accelerated in 1931 when business was down 27%. By 1932, business was off 57% and it hit rock bottom in 1933 when it was down over 63%. Employees were cut, advertising was cut, and new attractions by 1933 were eliminated. Maintenance and entertainment weren't cut and somehow the Park survived.

Every year Kennywood took out a loan from its bank in March to open the Park, paying it back by June 15. In 1933 Kennywood was unable to arrange a loan at the bank. The Park management had to ask employees to take a voluntary wage cut which would be repaid to them on June 15. McSwigan and Henninger were able to borrow some money on their own. They put it into the Park and it opened.

(Prior page) The Bug House was very popular during the Great Depression because one small admission could provide hours of fun. It had all the traditional amusement park devices, like Human Roulette Wheels, Revolving Barrel, Vibrating Floor, etc.

"For free" was the name of the game in the early 1930's. The Park offered a free playground, hoping that people who would be attracted by it would spend some of their money in the Park. Note in the background the double dip of the Pippin.

In 1930 the Park opened a free Menagerie which featured common non-exotic animals.

A long-term Kennywood favorite was another free attraction in the 1930's. At the end of each season the monkeys were shipped "home" (in crates) to their suppliers who would refund part of their "rental" fee to the Park.

67

Above: An Amusement Park cannot simply build a refreshment stand. It has to build its refreshment stands with "character." Kennywood's new stand built near the Pippin and the Bug House had an individuality all its own.

Below: Kennywood had a Penny Arcade as early as the 1910's, but with the development of new machines like skee-ball arcades really came into their own in the 1930's.

Many industries and schools in Western Pennsylvania cancelled picnics, so competition for the remaining picnics became cut-throat. A picnic war developed among amusement parks in Eastern Ohio and Western Pennsylvania. Some unscrupulous park men offered picnic committees extravagant gifts. Gold watches and silver cups were given. Some parks even offered cash rebates of up to $1,000 which the picnic committee could use as it saw fit.

Picnic committees swelled in size, with some reaching as many as 40 members. These large committees traveled from park to park accepting free gifts and admissions. Free "special" entertainment and liquor were further inducements.

Although attendance at the remaining picnics was large, spending was way down. The roller coasters, known as high ticket rides, traditionally charged the most for admission, and their attendance decreased the most. If someone had only a dollar to spend, he would spread it out on the ten cent or five cent rides.

One of the cheapest attractions in the early 1930's was the Bug House. People would pay fifteen cents and spend all day in the old Fun House. It was almost impossible to get in the Fun House after 1:00 p.m. This led to the conversion of the Bug House into a skooter ride in 1935.

Business also fell off for games and souvenirs. Kennywood cashiers were surprised how many welfare checks were cashed at the Park. Many people spent the day at the Park when there wasn't anything else to do.

Left: Good-looking girls on the beach were always good publicity for the Park.

Below: The giant swimming pool remained a major attraction in the 1930's although the admission price had to be dropped. Note the use of American Flags on the grandstand. The Park had over a hundred American Flags decorating its buildings.

Top: Park management offered another free playground, this one in connection with the Swimming Pool.

Above: The slightly tattered swim suits on this bevy of beauties suggests the depression conditions of the 1930's.

Kennywood's advertising shifted from shining new rides to free attractions. There were free monkeys, free circus acts, free play equipment, free parking, free Sunday band concerts, and free miniature menageries stocked with animals and birds.

Brady McSwigan commented in a letter in February 1932 that "working conditions in Pittsburgh are bad. There is much destitution and naturally, since the working man has had many days of unemployment, I cannot see how we can expect good business." The steel mills that ringed Kennywood were strangely clean and silent.

Prices for the big pool were reduced to thirty-five cents for adults and twenty cents for children. The coasters were reduced from twenty-five cents to fifteen cents.

In 1933, Kennywood's restaurant offered a box lunch with a ham and cheese sandwich, a roast beef sandwich, a square iced cake, one apple, and a small pie for fifteen cents, or a ham and cheese sandwich, a roast beef sandwich, ham sandwich on a bun, a square iced cake, an apple, a ½-pint bottle of chocolate milk, and a small pie for twenty-five cents.

To help pay the bills during the winter, Kennywood offered roller skating in the dance pavilion in 1934. The park bought roller skates and a new public address system. Skating cost twenty-five cents in the afternoon and thirty-five cents in the evening and

Above: The Park added a dark ride (Laugh-In-The-Dark) by Harry Traver in 1930. This ride replaced the Dodgem which was sold.

Left: Pretty girls, a boat, and a beautiful day. Who could ask for more?

Below: Picnics were even more popular in the 1930's when many people couldn't afford to eat in the Park's Restaurant.

Left: Kennywood's famous birthday cake made its first appearance in 1931. For years thereafter it was up-dated with one new candle each year.

Below: Long a Kennywood landmark, the Floral Calendar leaves no doubt on what date a picture is taken, such as this one on 28 May 1934.

WATCHING THE FREE CIRCUS AT KEN

on weekends. Ice skating on the lagoon was also tried for a short time.

An electric auto ride and Laff in the Dark were purchased from Harry Traver in 1930. Traver's ride firm, which built more rides for Kennywood in the 1920's and early 1930's, went into receivership in 1933. Kennywood planned to have Traver build a major new roller coaster in 1932 or 1933 but the Depression and later World War II caused these plans to be scrapped.

The auto ride and miniature railroad replaced the Pony Track next to Kiddieland. The Pony Track was moved next to the Racer.

The auto ride had 12 little cars which each rider could control within wooden side walls. The ride originally had small hills, but they were removed in the 1940's because many rear-end collisions were caused when some cars couldn't get over the hills on rainy days.

The old Dodgem ride was remodeled into a Laff in the Dark ride. Laff in the Dark was an 825-foot long dark ride in which people traveled in small two-seat cars. These two rides were the last major rides Kennywood bought until 1935.

Kennywood installed a Tom Thumb Miniature Golf Course in 1930 to take advantage of the miniature golf craze. It also added a golf school and driving range in the free parking area, but receipts for the driving range didn't measure up to expectations and it only lasted one season.

To stimulate attendance, McSwigan and Henninger brought in a wild west show rodeo in 1931 just as had been done in 1906. The rodeo played from July 3 to August 8 in an especially constructed arena in the free parking area.

The Compton-Hughes Great Wild West Rodeo was headed by Colonel "Cy" Compton and Captain Jack Hughes. Colonel Compton, known as "King of the Cowboys," had originally been a member of Buffalo Bill's Troupe. Captain Hughes for four consecutive seasons had been the champion bronco riding cowboy of the Northwest. The show had 45 champion cowboys, cowgirls, Seminole Indians, 40 wild horses, and 20 genuine Brahman steers. The sixteen-act show cost thirty-five cents for adults and twenty-five cents for children.

Kennywood's famous birthday cake was "baked" first in 1931. It stood five feet high, twenty feet in diameter, and originally had 33 candles. Each year a new candle was added.

The floral basket, calendar, and elephant were added to the landscaping in 1931. The rock garden was added in 1934.

In the bandshell, Danny Nirella, Cervone's Redcoats, Vantine, Pittsburgh Railways Company Band, and Joseph Nirella appeared. The nationality day committees also used the stage. The Park held an amateur contest with the winner receiving a two-week booking at the Stanley Theater in Pittsburgh.

A panoramic view of Lake Kennywood in 1930, showing from left to right: The Dance Pavilion, The Ferris Wheel, The Bridge to the Island Stage (Pony Track in background), The Island Stage and the Kennywood Speaker, The Racer, some maintenance buildings, the Jack Rabbit, and the Boat Rental Stand.

The Auto Race was another ride by Harry Traver, of nearby Beaver Falls, Pennsylvania. It featured little electrically-driven cars styled after the Packard, the most prestigious automobile of the day. The cars originally had a windshield, headlights, and a "moto-meter." All of those accessories were removed in the 1930's to give these little cars a more streamlined look. The wooden track originally had three small hills, which were removed in the 1940's because of rear-end collisions. Note the electrical pick-up bar on the side of the car.

A miniature golf craze swept across the country in the early 1930's, and Kennywood Park, taking advantage of this development, installed a "Tom Thumb" course. The course was located in the area between the Trolley Station and the old merry-go-round building which had been converted to a refreshment stand.

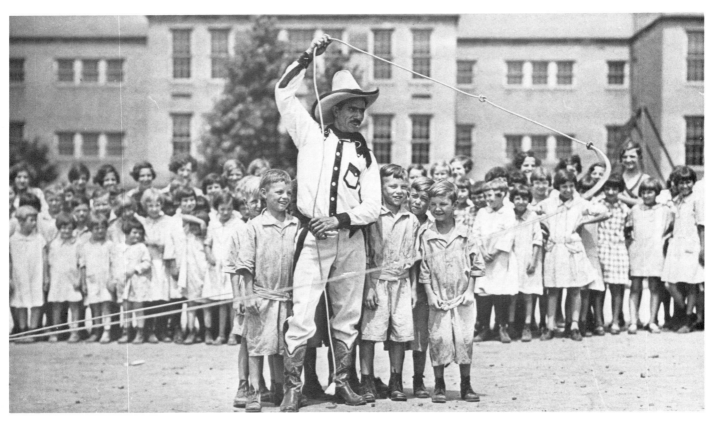

Colonel "Cy" Compton, owner of the Compton-Hughes Great Wild West Rodeo Show.

COMPTON-HUGHES
GREAT WILD WEST RODEO
Kennywood Park . July 3rd to Aug. 8th

ADVERTISING COURTESY

ADMIT ONE

Good Only 1931

MANAGEMENT RESERVES THE RIGHT TO REFUSE ADMISSION
FOR ABUSE OF COURTESY OR ANY OTHER CAUSE .... MANAGER

To promote business during the Depression, Kennywood brought a "Wild West" Rodeo to the Park in 1931. The performers were required to make trips into the local communities to lasso potential customers. The show, which was originally to last one month, was held over an extra month. During Prohibition management had less difficulty with the mixing of alcohol and the performers than was the case two decades earlier with the previous Wild West Show.
A special arena had to be constructed for the rodeo on the Athletic Field, across the highway from the main park.

Dancing remained a good source of revenue in the early 1930's. Bands like Harvey Marburger's appeared nightly except Sunday in the Kennywood Dance Pavilion. A few of the promotional fliers that were sent out advertising the forthcoming bands appear below.

In 1934, Kennywood broadcast several nationality days over KQV Radio. However, it was discontinued because the station didn't know what was being said and someone in the band used the phrase "go to hell" on one broadcast.

The following notice was posted on the bandstand: "Kennywood wouldn't tolerate anything said or done on this stage that is indecent or is off color in any sense of the word. This Park is a family institution. Performers are not permitted to sing any song or use any gag that is not 100% strictly clean. A representative of the Park attends all concerts and will hear the entire performance."

Kennywood's most popular free stage act, the Zachinni's Human Cannonball, appeared for the first time in 1931. "Braving death Zachinni fearlessly allows himself to be belched forth from the mouth of a 'Big Bertha' and catapulted through space. A drawing card unequalled in the annals of show history." Over the years this act proved to be the best drawing circus act Kennywood offered.

Other acts that appeared were Dave Castillo's Riding Circus, Sensational Jacks, Robinson's Elephants, Flying Melzora's (Quintelle of Aerialists), and Looping Nixes in Their Globe of Death.

To increase the efficiency and volume of the "Voice of Kennywood," the Park's own internal radio, a new Music Tower was constructed in 1930 on the spectacular stage of the Island in the Lagoon.

In the picture above the Dance Pavilion was still open, but it was enclosed during the 1934 season when the Park offered winter roller skating. However, roller skating never proved to be very popular, and was discontinued after a few seasons.

Below: No major new rides were added between 1930 and 1935, but in this picture can be seen some of the rides built in the 1920's—The Tumble Bug, The Seaplanes, and the Pippin.

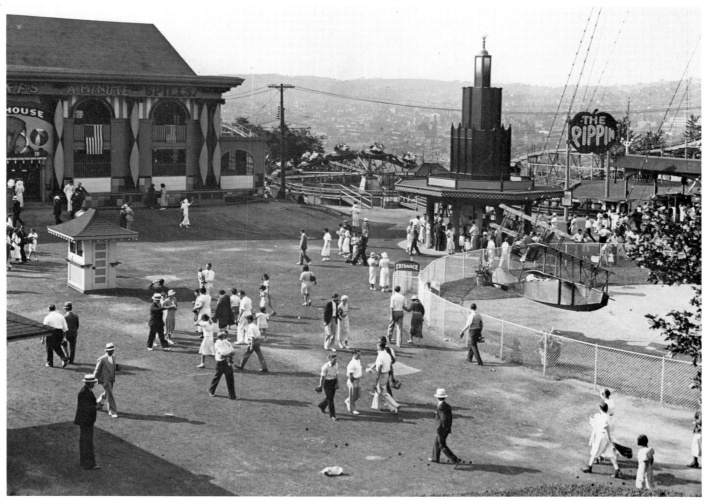

Mary's Garden was originally Mary Mary Quite Contrary's Garden. The idea was borrowed from Playland at Rye, New York. This garden survived into the 1970's. For the Republicans, a floral elephant made of "Hen-And-Chickens" was added.

A bevy of beautiful Marys in Mary's Garden.

Fun on The Farm was a small carnival type ride, purchased by the Park in 1934. For every 10 Popsicle sticks, a patron received one ride ticket. Over 25,000 sticks were received in 1933!

The Amos and Andy Radio Show was so popular that Kennywood Park broadcast it nightly from 7:00 p.m. to 7:15 p.m. over the Voice of Kennywood. *The Voice of Kennywood* publication, edited by Rosey Roswell, also became the name of a four-page folder printed in two colors which the Park would circulate bi-monthly to 1,500 readers. *Kennywood Illustrated News* was first reduced to four pages and then was discontinued in 1932.

Brady McSwigan was upset with the new styles in bathing suits and his comments were printed December 15, 1932, in the *Pittsburgh Catholic*. He wanted the manufacturers to know that swimming pool owners didn't care for "such indecencies as the modern bathing suit bring." "Current tendency in bathing suits has already gone too far," he said.

An Ice Day promotion was held in 1932. A number of local ice companies gave away free tickets with every ice delivery. These special tickets were good only on ice day. Ice companies provided displays of ice sculptures, ice houses, and the use of ice. Special "ice races" were held in the athletic field.

Penny pitch game was added in 1931. In this game the bell rang when a penny hit the right spot. There were skee ball, dart shooting at balloons, a shooting gallery, and balls thrown at milk bottles.

A group of Kiddieland pictures, showing that the area remained basically unchanged in the early 1930's. The only major addition was a Kiddie Tickler Ride, built by W. F. Mangels, shown at the right.

In 1933, a Popsicle Day was held at the Park. Kids all over the Pittsburgh area saved popsicle sticks. For every ten sticks, one ride ticket was given. Over 25,000 popsicle sticks were redeemed.

Kennywood purchased two used rides for 1931 and 1934. They were a Chair-O-Plane swing in 1931 and a portable type dark ride called Fun on the Farm in 1934. This small dark ride was located between the Jack Rabbit and Racer.

In 1931 a five-car tickler or miniature Virginia Reel was purchased for Kiddieland. This ride, built by Mangels, was the first Kiddie Tickler ride built.

The major addition in 1933 was a Mouse City containing 300 white rodents. An old refreshment stand measuring 8' x 11' was converted at a cost of $145. This attraction proved so popular that the National Amusement Park Association issued a special bulletin in 1933.

The Park held a Roosevelt Day in honor of Franklin Roosevelt in 1934. It was a good omen because business turned up in 1934. The government was involved in the unemployment and monetary system. Some money was available, banks were no longer closing, and slowly the large industrial plants came back. Fortunately, the second half of the 1930's was a good period for steel and other heavy industries and Kennywood prospered.

The narrow escape of 1933 wasn't soon forgotten and Kennywood wasn't about to resume the heavy growth rate of the 1920's.

The Railroad built by the Dayton Fun House was moved next to the Auto Race in 1930. A new facade in a similar style to that for the Auto Race was constructed, and a locomotive and other railway scenes were painted on it. The original third rail electric locomotive was re-styled to resemble a steam locomotive.

The Kennywood Refreshment Company was a separate partnership, and later a corporation, that ran the Kennywood Restaurant and food stands. The picture above shows the restaurant with tables completely set with sparkling linens. The picture below shows the old Carousel Pavilion after it had been converted to a Refreshment Stand.

All Highways Lead To Kennywood

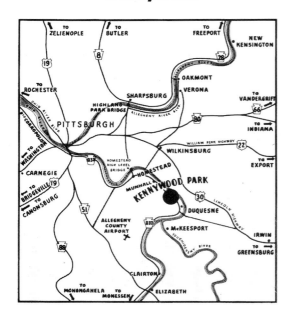

Mary Call measured the length of rides on the merry-go-round with an egg timer.

With business looking up in 1934, Kennywood held a Roosevelt Day in honor of Franklin D. Roosevelt, the thirty-second President of the United States. The Park used its big book for a Franklin Roosevelt tribute. The Park has used this same book for other presidents and various organizations.

6

The Big Band Era

(Previous page) Probably the most identifiable symbol for Kennywood Park is its Noah's Ark Dark Walk-thru. It was constructed in 1936, the same year the Pittsburgh suffered its most devastating flood.

(Above) The thirties were the greatest period of popularity of the "Big Bands." Kennywood featured local bands, regional bands like Moore-Stump, as well as ones with a national reputation.

"And now, live and direct from Kennywood's Dance Pavilion at Kennywood—the musical sounds of Tommy Tucker!" During the 1930's and 1940's, hundreds of bands were broadcast from Kennywood over radio station WCAE. Later KDKA, KQV, and WWSW were also used.

The summer was traditionally a slow time in network broadcasting and local stations were permitted to originate dance bands in the afternoons and evenings. WCAE originated dance bands live from Kennywood, first over the NBC Basic Red Network and later over Mutual and American Broadcasting Network.

In the early 1930's, these live remote broadcasts had few rules. The primary one was to play loudly, but as radio broadcasting became more sophisticated engineers started to control the broadcast.

In 1935 Ford Billings, general manager of radio station WCAE, wrote Brady McSwigan that "our engineer spent about three hours yesterday on a slight rearrangement of the position of the members of the orchestra before the microphone; and I am sure if you will compare the results, you will agree that he has made quite a decided improvement."

The stations provided an announcer and script for continuity on the broadcast. Here is part of a script for a Tommy Tucker broadcast from Kennywood in 1938:

Announcer—Music in Tommy Tucker time . . . and again . . . pretty Amy Arnell at our microphone to grace this next selection with her charming voice. Amy sings while Tommy and the orchestra play . . . "I haven't anyone till you."

Music—"I hadn't anyone till you."

Announcer—A cardiac quotation in the style of Tommy Tucker! . . .

The Dance Pavilion was remodeled and redecorated in Art-deco style in 1936. The orchestra stage was enlarged to accommodate the large national dance bands. All illumination was made indirect with no exposed lights. A new music amplification system was added, which brought sound to every corner of the dance floor. It was described as "one of the finest and most beautiful ballrooms of the nation. Expense was not even considered in transforming the huge building into a comfortable and eye-appealing vision of decorative enchantment."

The Park adopted the Art Deco style for their Dance Pavilion in 1936. The management bragged about their indirect lighting system to the point where not one light bulb was visible! Band promotion pictures were common during the big band era; in the shot below one of the band leaders was photographed on the lion of the beautiful Dentzel carousel.

FLASH NEWS...
to Kennywood Dancers

*L*ast season Kennywood promised great dance bands. The big Dance Pavilion gave you Rudy Vallee, Don Bestor, Ted Fio Rito, Tommy Tucker, Jimmy Joy, Ace Brigode and a host of others. **For 1937 a still greater schedule of orchestra attractions will be presented.** Nearly all have never played Kennywood before. Wait and see what is in store for our dance patrons.

Keep this announcement for dates

| Sat. Eve. May 1 **VAL GARVIN** AND HIS POPULAR ORCHESTRA | Sat. Eve. May 8 **JESS HAWKINS** AND HIS ORCHESTRA |

Starting Saturday, May 15th

FAMOUS PHIL LEVANT AND HIS ORCHESTRA
43 weeks at Chicago's celebrated Bismark Hotel A coast-to-coast Network favorite direct from the Gibson Hotel, Cincinnati.

13 Great Musicians, with the lovely GRETCHEN LEE and GEORGE WALD, Vocalists

This flier was published in 1937.

DANCING - For the Grownups there will be Dancing Afternoon and Evening in the remodeled and redecorated Pavilion with
Will Roland and his Orchestra

On the opposite page is the Racer Coaster. Notice the dress of the patrons, including the man in the car on the right who wears his hat! The cars travel much of the course close enough to each other that riders can touch people in the other car.
Above: Few coasters today can match the beauty of the entryway to Kennywood's Coaster.
Below: A large "electric fountain" and special outdoor lighting was added in the late 1930's.

Boys and Girls

JUNE 11

HERE'S the DATE!
the BIGGEST EVENT OF THE YEAR

Your SCHOOL PICNIC at KENNYWOOD PARK

Take this Circular home and show it to your family

All will want to go along to enjoy the many pleasures provided at the Picnic.

THIS YEAR, YOUR OUTING WILL BE THE VERY BEST EVER!
There is ever so much more to see and "do" at the great Amusement Park.

There are new Rides, Beautiful New Buildings, enlarged facilities for your convenience and comfort. You will find KENNYWOOD decidedly more attractive and certainly more appealing than ever before.

HAVE FUN ON THE BRAND-NEW RIDEE-O   SEE THE STRATOSHIP

Don't miss the thrilling FREE SHOW on the enlarged Island Stage

AFT. 4:30 **FREE** EVE. 9:30 **LES KIMRIS** "Birds on the Wing" The Most Thrilling Aerial Performance Ever Presented	**DANCING** AFTERNOON and EVENING In The Beautiful Pavilion **BARRON ELLIOTT and his Orchestra**

Auspices: New Kensington Workingmen's Picnic Association
EVERYBODY INVITED TO ATTEND

BASKETS
All baskets will be checked at P.R.R. Station at New Kensington, Pa. (Except small boxes).

AMUSEMENT TICKETS
Tickets on sale Main Street School, Wednesday, June 8—Thursday, June 9 and Friday, June 10, at Second Ward and Walnut Street Schools at 7:00 P.M. Three for ten cents.

FREE AMUSEMENT TICKETS
Given to all school children on special trains, also those arriving by automobile coming in gate within free parking hours—10:30 A.M. to 2:00 P.M.

RAILROAD TICKETS
Only half fare coupons will be accepted from children under 12 years of age on special trains.
Children over 12 years of age must exchange their coupons and pay 30c for special round trip excursion tickets at High School and Main Street School Saturday, June 11, from 7:00 A.M. to 8:00 A.M.
Half fare coupons will not be accepted from children over 12 on special trains. (All Daylight Saving Time).

AUTOMOBILES—Free admittance and parking at Park until 2:00 P.M. Daylight Saving Time.

NOTICE! This is the only Picnic at Kennywood Saturday, June 11th.
Supply yourself with plenty of Amusement Tickets for a good time and save money. Positively no Amusement Tickets sold at Park at reduced price.   PICNIC COMMITTEE

SPECIAL TRAINS—All Daylight Saving Time
RAILROAD FARE—ADULTS 60c—CHILDREN 30c
ON SALE AT P. R. R. STATION

1st Section Lv. New Kensington........ 8:40 A. M.	**RETURNING**
2nd Section Lv. New Kensington........ 9:30 A. M.	Lv. Kennywood Park 8:00 P.M., 8:30 P.M., 10:30 P.M.
3rd Section Lv. New Kensington........10:30 A. M.	All trains stopping at Parnassus on return

Noah's Ark was positioned on Kennywood's Mount Ararat, and the picture shows how patrons originally entered it. Fun seekers entering the Ark had to cross tilting barrel tops. The man who blew the famous air hose to raise skirts can be seen at the left rear.

Amusement Park executives shown in a pugilistic pose at a Pennsylvania Amusement Park Association Meeting are (l to r) George H. Laverman, Carl E. Henninger (asst. general manager of Kennywood), Brady McSwigan (president of Kennywood) and Charles L. (Nip) Beares Jr. Brady McSwigan served as president of the Association in 1937.

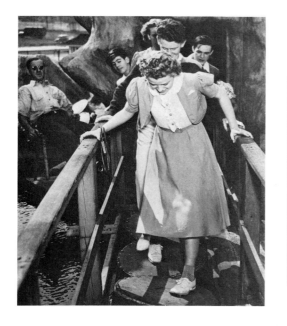

Closed for the season, under a beautiful but ominous sky. In the background is the new $35,000 office building.

During the Big Band Era of the 1930's and 1940's Kennywood used local, regional, and national bands.

Kennywood continued to use old favorites like Danny Nirella Cervone's Redcoats, and new bands like Jim Palmer, Brad Hunt, and Clyde Knight for free band concerts from the bandstand on Sunday as well as some dates in the Dance Pavilion.

Bands with regional reputations like Phil Levant, Jimmy Joy, Lee Barrett, Ace Brigoda, Art Kassal, Barron Elliot, Tommy Tucker, Jess Hawkins, and Lawrence Welk were featured in the Dance Pavilion for a week or two. These bands were eager to play at Kennywood for the network exposure.

Dance Pavilion regulations were very specific with dance evening sessions between 8:30 to 12:00. The orchestra was to play continuously the first half hour as music was broadcast over the Park's public address system. In the 1930's, no swing music was permitted and jitterbugging was discouraged in the 1940's. Bands were to play a minimum of fast tempo music, and waltzes were encouraged. No smoking on the bandstand or alcoholic beverages were permitted in the Dance Pavilion.

Kennywood also featured many of the big name bands like Ozzie Nelson, Benny Goodman, Vaughn Monroe, Harry James, Les Brown, and Rudy Vallee for one-night stands.

Rudy Vallee, who had been a radio star for years, appeared at Kennywood with his band "The Connecticut Yankees" July 15, 1936. The band came in by train from Cleveland the day of the engagement. One of F. W. Henninger's sons, Harry Henninger, was given the job of driving Rudy Vallee and his manager from the railroad station to the Park. The rest of the band rode in a bus while a truck carried their baggage.

As Vallee's party neared the Park, they ran into a tremendous traffic jam of people trying to get to the Park to hear Rudy Vallee. As 8:30 p.m. approached, impatient motorists started honking their horns. This upset Vallee, who finally stuck his head out the car window and said, "Stop your honking. You're coming to see me, and I haven't arrived yet." Unfortunately no one could hear him and the din continued.

Rudy Vallee and the other dance bands helped keep Kennywood's head above water during the early 1930's.

Noah's Ark was built in 1936 and helped keep Kennywood afloat. It is the most famous symbol of the Park for over 45 years.

Kennywood had wanted to build Noah's Ark as early as 1929 but the Depression got in the way. It is ironic that Noah's Ark was built in the same year that Western Pennsylvania suffered its worst flood.

The first thrill ride that literally turned its passengers upside down at Kennywood was the Loop-O-Plane by Eyerly Aircraft Corp. of Salem, Oregon. Only the brave would submit to this stomach-unsettling experience! The ride was installed in 1936.

Noah's Ark proved to be so popular that Kennywood built a second walk-thru in 1937, 13 Spook Street. It was built next to the Jack Rabbit. Two games stands were built on to the old Haunted Castle. The first Games in those stands were the Electro Ball and the Auto Game.

Bottom: Kennywood Park has always been beautiful at night, and by the late 1930's photographic film was fast enough to capture the lights. In this picture can be seen the lights of the Circle Swing, The Restaurant, and in the foreground, the Refreshment Stand. All of these were beautifully reflected in Lake Kennywood.

95

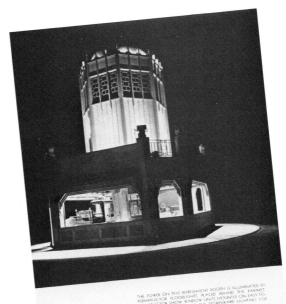

THE TOWER ON THIS REFRESHMENT BOOTH IS ILLUMINATED BY PERMAFLECTOR FLOODLIGHTS PLACED BEHIND THE PARAPET. PERMAFLECTOR SHOW WINDOW UNITS MOUNTED ON EASY-TO-INSTALL CONDUIT PROVIDED THE DOWNWARD LIGHTING FOR THE REFRESHMENT AREA.

THE UPPER PORTION OF THE PENNY ARCADE IS FLOODLIGHTED FROM ABOVE THE SIGN. FLOODLIGHTS DIRECTED HORIZONTALLY TO THE BUILDING FROM THE MARQUEE SILHOUETTES BOTH THE SIGN AND THE MARQUEE. PERMAFLECTOR UNITS BEHIND THE MARQUEE FLOODLIGHT THE CORNER PYLONS. PERMAFLECTORS EQUIPPED WITH ROUNDELS LIGHT THE ENTRANCE.

A WEIRD EFFECT IS ACHIEVED BY DIRECTING A GREENISH-BLUE LIGHT FROM A BANK OF PERMAFLECTOR UNITS ON THE ROCKS. UPON WHICH HORSES ARE SILHOUETTED. THE ENDS AND BOTTOM PORTION OF THE ARE ILLUMINATED FROM PERMAFLECTORS CONCEALED BEHIND THE ROCKS. A SERIES OF SMALL PERMAFLECTORS AT THE BASE OF THE CABIN ILLUMINATE THE UPPER PORTION OF THE ARE. A DOWNLIGHT FROM CONCEALED LOUVERED PERMAFLECTOR ADDS TO THE EERIE EFFECT.

PERMAFLECTORS EQUIPPED WITH ROUNDELS RECESSED OVER THE SIX ENTRANCES TO THE PENNY ARCADE PROVIDE BRILLIANT AND INVITING ILLUMINATION.

A SERIES OF PERMAFLECTORS MOUNTED IN THE CEILING BEHIND THE VALANCE LIGHT THE BAND STAND. THE DECORATIVE SIDE ILLUMINATION IS ACCOMPLISHED BY LIGHTS INSTALLED BEHIND EACH OF THE FINS.

Kennywood made extensive use of both flood-lighting and indirect lighting during the 1930's. The Park also used fireworks to attract patronage; note the picture below.

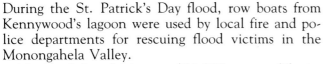

During the St. Patrick's Day flood, row boats from Kennywood's lagoon were used by local fire and police departments for rescuing flood victims in the Monongahela Valley.

Noah's Ark, which cost $20,000, was a life-size boat built on a mount surrounded by one foot of water. The boat contained a rippling floor, a jail from which one escaped via rubber bars and a growling stuffed bear. The boat rocked back and forth with a fog horn sounding an ominous note. Air jets were located strategically along the path leading to the Ark with one jet placed just inside the door. Girls still wore skirts during the 1930's and 1940's, making the entrance of the Ark one of Kennywood's most popular attractions.

Kennywood broadcast the screams and shouts from Noah's Ark over its public address system. One night Brady McSwigan said it sounded like the roar of the Army-Navy Football Game.

A Loop-O-Plane by Eyerly Aircraft Company of Salem, Oregon, was also added in 1936. It featured rocket planes which held eight adults and went around and around looping the loops.

The next generation started working at Kennywood full time when Carl Henninger, F. W. Henninger's son, became assistant manager in 1936. Brady McSwigan was instrumental in the founding of the Pennsylvania Amusement Park Association and he became its President in 1938.

The Teddy Bear, a Junior Coaster, was designed by Herbert Schmeck of the Philadelphia Toboggan Company. Brady McSwigan, Kennywood's president, had seen a similar coaster at Coney Island, Cincinnati, Ohio, and he obtained the plans and built the coaster in 1935. It featured a gentle double dip.

Kennywood was and still is the best school picnic Park in the United States. Here is a school picnics' brochure from 1937:

"A few days before your picnic the Kennywood ticket man will come to your school room and sell special reduced rate amusement tickets. Save some pennies and buy yourself tickets at a big savings as this is the only chance to get these tickets at a little more than half price. 5 cent value tickets will be sold for 3 cents. A big strip of 5 cent tickets is 15 cents. 4 free amusement tickets to each student. All will go in a special street car. For the grown ups there will be dancing afternoons and evenings with Jess Hawkins and his famous orchestra."

An electric fountain was added to the swimming pool in 1937. The Kiddie Mill, which was designed by Herb Schmeck of Philadelphia Toboggan Company, was built in Kiddieland and a fire truck and pony cart ride were purchased.

The Park's advertisements said See The Strat-O-Ship; they didn't say Ride The Strato-O-Ship. The Strat-O-Ship was another ride not for the faint hearted! The ride, built by R. E. Chambers, was a direct result of the Buck Rogers mania of the 1930's. Notice the little propellor on the back of the ship.

99

Linen post cards of Kennywood Park.

(Opposite) The second major ride purchased by Kennywood in 1938 was the Ridee-O. It cost $8,200 and was built by the Spillman Engineering Corporation of North Tonawanda, New York. It was an 18-car model and is the forerunner of today's Himalaya-type ride.

Noah's Ark had been so successful that another walk-thru, 13 Spook Street, was added. It replaced Fun on the Farm on a spot between the Jack Rabbit and Racer. The Spook Street Castle had comic spooks and a magic carpet conveyor belt ride which carried people to the exit.

The motion picture theater was removed and the Penny Arcade expanded to occupy the whole building. At the opposite end of the Park an ultra-modern Sportland Building with three amusement games was added.

A two-story picnic pavilion was built next to the Jack Rabbit. Special night illumination was added to the swimming pool, Penny Arcade, Sportland Building, tower refreshment stand, skooter building, Noah's Ark, and 13 Spook Street.

For 1938, the Island Stage was enlarged and one of the most sensational acts to appear during the 1930's were the Kimirs. They were a family aerial act from Germany. Kennywood had trouble booking this act because replies to their inquiries were in German.

After three or four years of recovery 1937 was another down year. The Park purchased a Ridee-O from Spillman Engineering Company of North Tonawanda, New York, and a Strat-O-Ship from R. E. Chambers Company which had a small Buck Rogers type ship on a large arm. Kennywood purchased new skooter cars from Lusse. They were painted a poppy red, trimmed with aluminum touched with a yellow stripe.

Here are some of the ticket prices in 1937: Children's rides and the Merry-Go-Round were 5 cents, and for 10 cents you could go on the Ridee-O, Laff in the Dark, Old Mill, Whip, Tumble Bug, Miniature Railroad, Auto Race, Caterpillar, or Sea Plane. It cost 15 cents for Spook Street, Noah's Ark, Skooter, Jack Rabbit, Pippin, Tom Thumb, and Loop-O-Plane. The Strat-O-Ship was 20 cents and the Boat on the Lake was 25 cents. The Swimming Pool cost 40 cents for adults and 25 cents for children.

Many of the gravel sidewalks were replaced by concrete or asphalt in 1938 and 1939.

Erwin Vettel, who had helped build Kennywood's first figure-eight coaster, returned as master mechanic in 1936. In 1938 Kennywood had 280 seasonal employees. H. D. Mansfield was the Voice of Kennywood. There were 118 ride operators, 122 refreshment employees, 37 in games and arcades, 43 in maintenance, 57 cashiers, and 20 in parking, rest rooms, and check rooms. Women employees only worked 54 hours a week while men worked 70.

The Park was still having trouble with skimpy bathing suits but in 1937 a representative of Jantzen Knitting Mills said that he thought the ultimate had been reached in women's bathing suits.

Receipts were down 25% in 1938 and Brady McSwigan complained about "a real shortage of money." This secondary down turn scared Kennywood and expansion again slowed down in 1938.

The Depression was over by 1939 but events in Europe and the Far East would soon have a big impact on America's economy. Pittsburgh's industry was shifting to a war footing. World War II would have a profound effect on Kennywood because money was plentiful but soon everything else would be rationed and hard to get.

Park Management decided to do away with the Bug House in 1934. Then replaced it with a Skooter Ride from Lusse Brothers Inc. of Philadelphia, Pennsylvania. Employees of the Park modified the building and related electrical equipment. The 20 cars cost $375 each for a total of $7500.

The Windmill was on a small island in Lake Kennywood. It was built in 1929 and remained on this island until 1940. It was then moved to a spot near the main entrance. The Cuddle-up was purchased from the Philadelphia Toboggan Company in 1935. It remained in the Park for only a few years.

7

The War Period

Kennywood's course from 1940 to 1945 was controlled by World War II. Priorities, war bonds, air raids, blackouts, shortages, gas rationing, the draft, and Navy Relief Fund became part of the Kennywood employee's vocabulary. Patriotic slogans like "Keep 'Em Flying," "Keep 'Em Rolling," and "Keep 'Em Fighting" were commonplace in the *Voice of Kennywood* pamphlet.

There were some material shortages in 1940, but Kennywood was able to move Traver's old Circle Swing to an island in the lagoon. The Windmill was removed and a foundation with 110 yards of concrete was poured to support the Swing's 49-ton steel tower. The Swing's old deluxe seaplanes were replaced with new rocket ships manufactured by R. E. Chambers. Since the rockets replaced small seaplanes, the rockets were three seater rather than the four-seater found in most other amusement parks.

Erwin Vettel, chief mechanic, commented on how amusement park construction in the 1940's contrasted to that in the old days. "In the old days when one wanted to build a refreshment stand all he needed was a saw horse, unplaned lumber and the American flag. Now such a stand is the work of a contractor, who sometimes employs an architect to design the

The superstructure of the old circle swings was moved to the island in Lake Kennywood, and placed on 110 yards of concrete. The old framework was covered with sheet metal and new tubing. New "modern" rocket ships were purchased from R. E. Chambers.

(overleaf)
This photo of Kennywood Park during World War II shows the new circle swing, called the Rockets on an island in Lake Kennywood, and the flying Skooter ride located in front of the regular Skooter. Note the large American Flag between the Carousel and the Restaurant.

Left: Flying Scooters were purchased from Bish-Rocco Company of Chicago, Illinois, during World War II. The little ships were painted in an Army Air Force motif.

Below: By the 1940's the restaurant had been enclosed, and a new awning entrance had been added.

building, and a construction engineer to put it up. An electrical engineer is called in to design scientifically the proper lighting effects. Plastics and new materials are used, chromium and glass in streamline effects. Lastly, it is colored with water colors. It's very different than when I started."

The park bought the Flying Scooter from Bisch-Rocco of Chicago, Illinois. The ride called the Dipsy Doodle replaced the seaplanes in front of Noah's Ark. It featured 10 two-seater airplanes on which the rider could control the height by an aileron.

A mechanical laughing man was inserted in the front of Noah's Ark. A recording permitted him to laugh from early in the morning till late at night.

There were 25 ponies and horses used for the pony track located next to the Racer with 33-year-old Buddy being the oldest. Washington Wentzel still headed up Kennywood's restaurant and 18 refreshment stands. In 1940 a juicy, tender filet mignon full-course deluxe dinner was offered in the restaurant for $2.

Kennywood was lucky enough to buy a Cuddle-Up which had been used at the New York World's Fair. It was becoming increasingly difficult to obtain new

amusement rides, as most amusement ride companies had converted their production over to war production. Copper, wire, lumber, and machine parts were very hard to obtain. Kennywood called its Cuddle-Up the Snapper and placed it in a building between the Whip and Shooting Gallery and across from the Dipsy Doodle.

13 Spook Street was rethemed by the Philadelphia Toboggan Company and became the Daffy Klub. The first name chosen was Laff Cafe but it seemed too similar to Laff In The Dark. Daffy Klub was advertised to be "A great big time for all." It was "Scair Conditioned" with music by "Nick Elodians" and "Silli Simp Fonnie."

The Music Plaza Bandstand was enlarged and restyled with white stucco and chrome trim. The Penny Arcade was enlarged and improved. In Kiddieland a new Roto Whip by F. W. Mangels of Coney Island was purchased.

In 1941 Slim Bryant and his Tri-State Barn Dance Show from KDKA radio was so popular it appeared three times in the music plaza. Dr. Jock Sutherland, head football coach of the NFL Brooklyn Dodgers, headed up the annual Scottish Clans of Western Pennsylvania picnic. Billy Conn, weighing only 174

The Daffy Klub replaced 13 Spook Street in 1941. A "magic carpet" which was a large human-sized conveyor belt moved the patron to the exit.

Pictured above are two stunts that were added to the Daffy Klub during World War II. The bulldog jumped at the patrons.

pounds, gave Joe Louis all he could handle in a heavy-weight championship fight which was broadcast over the *Voice of Kennywood* to Park patrons in 1941. A Nash sedan given away on Labor Day, 1941 was the last car given away until the end of World War II.

There were signs of War during the 1941 season. The Annual Polish Day had Admiral Standley as its speaker. He was a member of the committee to aid the Allies. Kennywood collected a ton of aluminum for defense by giving free ride tickets for every aluminum pot or pan.

Brady McSwigan, president of Kennywood, wanted to buy a new bubble bounce and Ferris wheel in October of 1941. He placed ads in *Billboard* for used rides but it was too late. Owners wouldn't part with rides and all amusement park ride production stopped when America entered the War in December 1941.

Carl E. Henninger, Frederick Henninger's son, became general manager of the Park in 1940. With the outbreak of War, he enlisted in the Navy. He served for the duration of the War in Kodiak, Alaska, which is about as far away from amusement parks as you can get.

Henninger wasn't the only Kennywood employee to serve in the armed forces. By December of 1942 there were 85 employees in the service, creating a terrible shortage of help. Many young men were hired who were soon drafted into the armed forces or took positions in defense industry.

Above: One of the figures on Noah's Ark gets a new coat of paint. Kennywood used over 600 barrels of paint yearly to dress up its stands and pavilions.

Left: Noah's Ark received a face-lifting in the 1940's when additional walkways were added on front of the attraction. A mechanical laughing man was added to the front of the mountain section, for additional ballyhoo.

More than members of the Kennywood family went to war, as thousands of young men enlisted or were drafted. Brady McSwigan commented, "The draft, of course, had its telling effect by July first (1942). Kennywood commenced to notice the cut in young men's patronage. Dancing and bathing were first to indicate that many boys had gone to serve Uncle Sam. Top flight bands such as Benny Goodman, Jimmy Dorsey, Charles Spivak and other lesser attractions failed to draw."

In Seattle, Washington, Pittsburgh district soldiers gathered around radios to listen to the Mutual Network broadcasts of bands live and direct from Kennywood. Private Roland Allard was chosen spokesman for the group. He wrote President McSwigan a letter of thanks on behalf of the boys when Charles Spivak's band at the park dedicated a number to Allard's Coastal Artillery over the Mutual Radio Network.

An Eli Wheel was added during the Second World War. Notice the small stars on the back of the seats and the flags used to decorate it. The sailor above may have been an expert on battleships, but at Kennywood he had to settle for a rowboat to entertain his girl.

Bottom: The Midway, from Whip to Kennywood Tower.

110

Maintenance remained important during the war. The life of many rides was extended by replacing a part here or a section there.

Kennywood, "The Nation's Greatest Picnic Park," was able to escape gas rationing and dimouts in 1942. However, a ban on chartered buses and trains hurt, causing the loss of more than 40 picnic outings. Although special trains were prohibited, regular trains continued to operate. The watchword was to "Give your neighbor a lift." One group from North Versailles, a town about seven miles from Kennywood, used a hay wagon drawn by two mules for transportation to the park.

Erwin A. Vettel, a great roller coaster builder in his own right and mechanical superintendent at Kennywood since March 1936, died September 23, 1943. He was replaced by his son, Andy Vettel.

Frank L. Danahey became general manager when Carl Henninger entered the Navy. The old guard of Brady McSwigan and Frederick Henninger had to carry the load during the War. In 1942 Brady McSwigan's 74-year-old mother was honored at the annual employees' banquet. Rosey Rowswell emceed the tribute to Mrs. McSwigan.

With a shortage of automobile tires, Kennywood was fortunate to still have trolley service to the park. There were no toy balloons, foreign-made souvenirs, Oriental tumbling acts, or over-sweetened lemonade for the duration of the War.

Carl E. Henninger, Kennywood's general manager, served in the Navy from 1942 to 1945. Many other Kennywood employees also served in the Armed Forces.

The Windmill became a landmark, being visible from the Entrance and Braddock Road. The electrically-illuminated blades could be seen for long distances as they slowly revolved. Every few years the Park hired a special craftsman to repair and repaint their carousel horses.

The Laff-In-The-Dark was re-styled in the art-deco mode, but the same old stunts like the kicking mule continued to be used.

During the war the Park gave thousands of special complimentary tickets to men and women who were members of the Armed Forces, as seen at the left. Note the prominent U.S. imprint.

Numerous stories were told during the war to illustrate the tire shortage. One story was to the effect that since monkeys were hard to get during the War, Kennywood was thinking about putting a *brand new tire* in the monkey cage as a real curiosity.

Kennywood gave 10% of its receipts from Wednesdays to the Army and Navy Relief Fund. During the War the Park contributed tens of thousands of dollars and Brady McSwigan served as a sub-chairman for the Pittsburgh District of Navy Relief Fund.

Employees purchased war bonds and war stamps. Since automobiles were in short supply, Kennywood gave war bonds for Labor Day giveaway.

During the war, Kennywood's slogan was changed from "Bigger and Better" to "Better but No Bigger." To get even simple repairs made, Kennywood had to apply for a priority rating on multi-paged forms to the Chief Amusement Section Service Equipment Division in Washington. Kennywood's maintenance department did an unbelievable job holding together a caterpillar that was over 20 years old and a tumble bug and whip which were over 15 years old.

Service men and women of the United States Army, Navy, Marines and Coast Guard in uniform were given a complimentary book of 20 amusement tickets entitling them to the admission on any 20 rides except the ponies, boats, pool, and evening dancing. Half-rate privileges were extended to service personnel for the swimming pool, and evening dancing.

Kennywood encouraged visits of service personnel but soldiers who wanted to show off their new skills with a rifle were often disappointed. Shooting gallery ammunition was rationed. In 1942 Kennywood could only get 70% of the 22 short cartridges it used in 1940. In order to get more ammunition, John F. McTighe, shooting gallery manager, wrote Washington that, "90% of the draft age boys have never held a rifle in their hand. In my opinion all the shooting galleries in this country are performing a much needed service in teaching the youth of this nation how to handle a rifle." Unfortunately, the War Board didn't grant relief until 1945.

In 1943 the *Voice of Kennywood* pamphlet published the following: "While we don't build tanks or fashion war tools, we do try to remake the man who makes the weapons used by our fighting forces on many fronts."

Kennywood sent a letter to its ex-employees in the Service keeping them informed on developments on the home front. In 1943 the letter commented that "you have perhaps heard the bad news that whiskey is now on the rationing list in Pennsylvania."

Kennywood had its first blackout in 1942 when the Park management decided to close for the evening. Civil defense regulations were then issued for the amusement park industry which included the following: "Under no circumstances should any person be allowed in a swimming pool during an air raid or air raid drill, whether during the day or night."

The Park had needed a new office building for years so in the late 1930's they build a new 2-story structure in art-deco or moderne style. The old service building next to it which contained rest rooms and a coat check area was modernized in a similar vein.

114

Above: The ballroom remained popular during World War II as regional and national shows originated there. Below: A distortion is a good way to check the seams in one's nylon hose! The extra length permits a closer inspection than usual.

Management was able to keep all of its roller coasters open during the war.

This Choo-Choo Miniature Railroad was purchased in 1945. Many a person remembers their first ride, as a child, on this fine ride.

116

Kennywood was divided into 5 air raid areas. The signal for a blackout was the playing of a special recording of "Old Black Joe" played on church chimes coupled with a special auto-call signal consisting of 17 short taps on the bells. Air raid wardens had special cupboards throughout the park, where they kept first aid supplies and necessary materials for fighting incendiary bombs and fires. Junior air raid wardens were to protect the cashiers in case of a blackout.

For 1944 the rides again were painted and reconditioned. The Dance Pavilion was restyled. When gas rationing was adopted for Western Pennsylvania in 1943, Kennywood advised, "Have your vacation at Kennywood—100 amusements." Over 2,000,000 complimentary tickets were given to service personnel during the war.

Kennywood purchased the Choo Choo Miniature Train which had been used at the World's Fair in 1939. Built by the Cagney Brothers, the streamline train, which was 36" gauge, had two locomotives and five eight-passenger cars. It was opened with a small track layout in 1945 and expanded in 1946 to a half mile in length.

The hardest problem faced by management during the War was getting personnel. Kennywood ran ads all during the war for ride operators, policemen, maintenance personnel, bookkeepers, cashiers, etc.

Herb Schmeck, general manager of the Philadelphia Toboggan Company, wrote Brady McSwigan that "during the 'thirties' Park men operated without any money most of the time and had very little financial background, and how during the 'Forties' they operate without help or help so inefficient that they can be classified as 'no help.'" Schmeck continued, "After the War, if Roosevelt is smart, he will can the New Dealers and bring in a group of Super Park executives to give him a lift and I am sure they would not do too bad a job of it at that."

After the War, Kennywood would not have time to run the government. It would have to use all its resources and energy to run its Park. With the coming of peace in 1945, new problems like continued material shortages, a baby boom, outdoor movies and television would appear.

Bobby-sox, saddle shoes, and french fries were the order of the day during the 1940's. Energy-efficient boats were a great way to get about on Lake Kennywood during pleasant summer days in years past.

Overleaf: The Midway as it appeared in July of 1946.

8

The Late 1940's: Growth Resumes

Overleaf: This Looper was one of the first of the new rides manufactured after World War II. The ride not only turned you over and over, but the cars also traveled around in a circle. The ride was purchased from the Allan Herschell Company; it was designed by Norman Bartlett.

After fifteen years of depression and war, Kennywood set about "modernizing" its buildings, rides, and fronts from 1946 to 1949, and in 1948 the Park had its first physical expansion since the 1920's.

Additions were made to the Administration Building and Service Building in 1946. An employees' cafeteria was added to the back of the restaurant and the restaurant was enclosed with windows after being open air for forty-eight years.

In 1946 Brady McSwigan commented in a letter to Herb Schmeck of Philadelphia Toboggan Company that peacetime wasn't easy. "This present era is really something. I have 98 more gray hairs since I last saw you."

A new facade done in the "World's Fair style" with lofty pylons was built for the Racer and adjoining rides. This new front was designed by Warren Hindenach of Philadelphia and was completed in spite of material shortages in 1946. A Bubble Bounce was purchased from Custer Specialty Company Inc. of Dayton, Ohio, for the space between the Pony Track and Racer.

Andy Vettel modified the homestretch of the Racer in 1949. The final hill, which had knocked out many a tooth over the years, was cut down. A new front for the Pippin was designed by Leo Kathe in 1949.

The old merry-go-round pavilion located adjacent to the street car loading station was completely redesigned in 1949. It had been turned into a refreshment stand in 1927. The exterior was modernized and its facade was embellished with yards and yards of neon tubing. The interior was made into an octagon shape, containing three food stands made of glass blocks and stainless steel.

The Little Choo Choo was expanded and a third locomotive was added in 1946. In 1947, it was found that the original World's Fair paint job advertising

Gimbels was bleeding through and the engines and cars had to be repainted. For years the train was run by C. W. Myers, a retired engineer from Braddock who had served 52 years on the Union Railroad.

In 1948, the Sportland Building was moved and the Teddy Bear Coaster dismantled. This formed a new mall with the Auto Ride, Choo Choo Train, and a new coaster—the Little Dipper—on one side, and the Sportland Building, skee ball alleys, and a shooting gallery on the other. A new ride, the Looper, with circular cages which seated two riders, was placed at the end of the mall near the Bandstand.

Twelve new skee ball alleys were purchased from the Philadelphia Toboggan Company. A new shooting gallery from W. F. Mangels was placed on the other side.

Ten new cars were bought for the Flying Scooter in 1949 and a Tilt-A-Whirl returned to Kennywood after many years absence. Inflation was a fact of life after World War II. Rides were more expensive with the Looper coasting $13,357, the Bubble Bounce $12,500, and the Tilt-A-Whirl $10,850.

Several modifications were made to the Racer in the late 1940's. They included a new facade and some changes in the track profile.

Below: A new mall area was developed in 1948 by Kennywood. This was the first major alteration to the Park's layout since the 1920's. Notice the Bandshell, the Looper, and the Little Dipper as they appeared on opening Sunday in 1948.

Voice of KENNYWOOD

A Friendly Greeting
to you every-so-often

from Kennywood Park
"Pittsburgh's Playground"

Vol. 16—No. 5   Edited by A. K. ("ROSEY") ROWSWELL   March 1946

COMES THE SPRING

WITH the first fall of snow last November the coming of Spring looked ages away—but like all good things, time brings its own rewards. Yes the dregs of winter still abide, but ere another issue of *Voice of Kennywood* reaches you, you will have glimpsed the golden daffodils nodding in the sunlight, lawns will be flashing their green velvet coverings, and the druggists will have disposed of their surplus mothballs.

Of a certainty Spring is beckoning. Soon the first pale blossom of the unripened year will be coloring the hillsides and offering the most convincing evidence of immortality. In the Spring one feels like shouting: *"Gee, it's great to be alive!"*

Always Spring brings a restless dissatisfaction with the past, and a renewed hope in the future. Always we are looking ahead to doing something big, and fine, and noble, and in that we have an asset more fundamental than all the wealth of the world. So long as we are inspired by that spirit, our future is secure. With that yen for improvement, we shall not go down to destruction, no matter how often we tremble "on the verge."

Ever since the crash of 1929 men have been predicting the end of America and the American way of life. You heard it on every hand during those trying days of 1941 through 1945. Then came the new year, and with it unrest in the ranks of labor and management. And again the end of America was predicted.

As long as we live in a country that will accept and sing such musical violations as "Chickery Chic, tra la, tra la," "Mairsy Doats," "The Hut Sut" and similar homocidal incentives, we're going to be all right—and a hundred thirty-five million people can't be wrong.

So, with Spring in the offing, lift your hearts and give thanks, for with it the world takes on new coloring, new promise, new opportunities. There is an invisible something in the Springtime that brings a softness to the air, and the lengthening days and twilight shadows are compensation after the rigorous weeks of winter.

Comes the Spring!

Along with the Looper, the Bubble Bounce was a new ride. Management had hoped to buy this Bubble Bounce in 1942, but the war interfered. Notice the lack of "flash" and decoration on the Bubble Bounce.

The voice of Kennywood was a small leaflet sent out by the Park from the early 1930's to the middle 1950's. It was edited by Rosey Rowswell, a famous Pirate baseball announcer of the day.

122

Spectators stand in awe of centrifugal force and its effects on patrons of the Hurricane, probably pondering if they should in turn "take the risk!"
The Shooting Gallery and New Games Building was built at the same time that the new mall was developed. Note the extensive use of neon lighting.

The Hurricane was probably the most disappointing ride that Kennywood has ever bought. After the success of the Looper, the Park bought the Hurricane, a Norman Bartlet-designed ride, from Allan Herschell Company in 1949. The ride had six cars suspended from rigid rotating arms. The cars could zoom 10° past horizontal but many patrons got sick on it. It also had maintenance problems when even the smallest foreign particles would disable the hydraulic system.

The cars were streamlined on the Travers Auto Ride, and new Tumble Bug cars resembling turtles were purchased from R. E. Chambers for the Tumble Bug.

Kennywood spent $615 for 41 thirty-second advertisements over WWSW Radio in 1946. Here is part of the script for one of these ads:

"Summertime is playtime, so make way for a full day of fun at Kennywood, Pittsburgh's foremost fun spot. Dozens of thrill-packed rides, playground facilities for the younger children, picnic grounds, inviting swimming pool and white sand beach, plus dancing in the pavilion to the music of Ray Herbeck's celebrated orchestra. Appearing on the Lagoon stage is Peaches and her Sky Revue . . . six girl aerial act. Be sure to spend at

least one great day of your vacation at Kennywood where there are thrills and entertainment for all. It's Kennywood . . . Kennywood Park. Remember, there will be a dazzling display of fireworks every night this week . . . and, your unused amusement tickets will be good this week through August 31."

Kennywood celebrated its Golden Anniversary season in 1947. The Park had celebrated its Silver Anniversary 24 years earlier but somewhere between the Silver and Gold it was decided to call 1898 the first season rather than 1899.

Kennywood still used its concrete cake for its Golden Anniversary celebration, but like a woman it quit putting on candles years before.

Danny Nirella's Redcoat Band was the featured attraction for the forty-second straight time in the Music Plaza. Free concerts were scheduled at 3 p.m. and 8 p.m.

A special banquet was held honoring the Park's Golden Anniversary. It was presided over by Brady McSwigan as president and Fred Henninger as secretary-treasurer. Fred Henninger had served as secretary-treasurer for 41 of the Park's 50 years.

Brady McSwigan served two terms (1946–1947) as president of the NAAPPB (National Association of Amusement Parks, Pools and Beaches). He followed in the footsteps of his father, Andy McSwigan, who had served three terms as the first president of this organization.

The main offices of Kennywood were located for many years in the Farmers Bank Building. Even during the season, Brady McSwigan and F. W. Henninger would spend the morning and early afternoon in the downtown office and then take the thirty-minute drive to the Park. Here they would stay until

Trolleys delivered many patrons to Kennywood, in this instance by a swift and comfortable P.C.C. car, during their golden anniversary season. The Park issued a souvenir brochure for its fiftieth anniversary season.

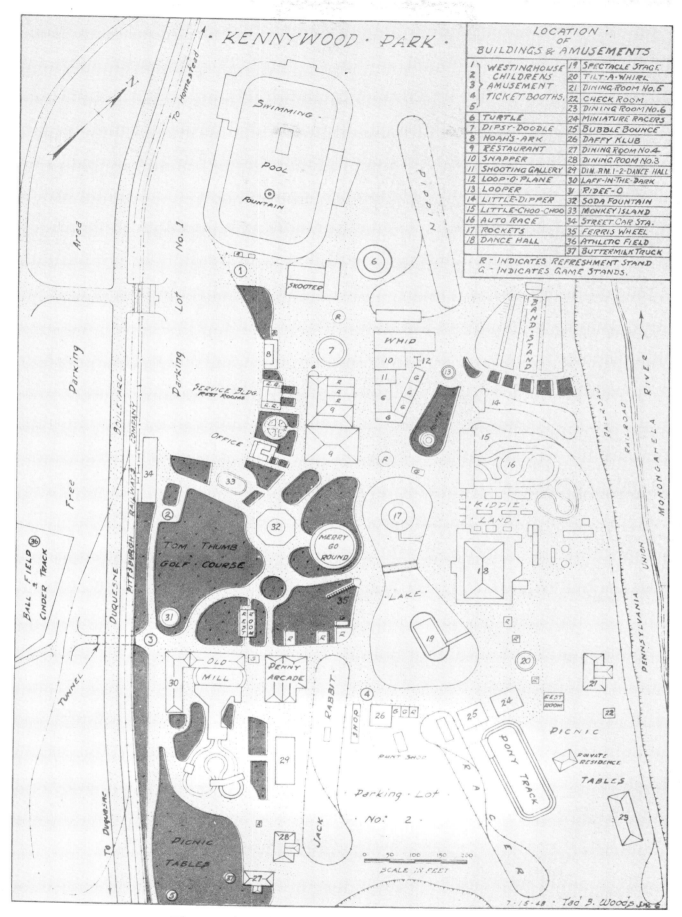

This map shows the layout of the Park as of July 15, 1948.

midnight. McSwigan was deathly afraid of fire so he would put the Park to bed before he would head for his home in Schenley Farms.

Washington M. Wentzel, who had been associated with the Park since 1903, died at 80 years of age in 1946. The previous May, Wentzel, who headed the Refreshment Company, prepared a banquet for 450 persons at the Park, not knowing he was to be honored until the guests were seated and he was informed the banquet was for himself.

A baby boom developed after World War II but Kennywood was ready with one of the biggest Kiddielands in the United States. Here is how Brady McSwigan described Kennywood's Kiddieland in a letter to a Denver park owner in 1947: "As to installing a Kiddieland, it has long been our feeling it was one of the most prudent installations we ever made. In 1924 we started out with the kiddie rides (all of Mangels manufacture), a carousel, whip, and swan ride. We have noticed that our kid layout has tended to build up our business, especially on Sundays and holidays. Our Kiddieland consists of a miniature whip, carrousel, auto ride, roto whip, "tickler" (miniature Virginia Reel), Ferris wheel, brownie coaster, boat ride (all of Mangels make), comet ride, pony ride of Pinto make, miniature seaplane swing (Uzzel make), fire engine (Allen Herschell make), little old mill designed by Herb Schmeck, chairplane, auto race and miniature railroad surrounding devices.

The Racer is one of the most beautiful roller coasters ever built. In this unusual aerial photograph the gorgeous symmetry of this fine ride is apparent. The new modern front, shown here as it neared completion, was finished in 1946.

126

Top: The Pippin had a unique lift which started after the coaster had already gone down two major hills. This feature was continued on the succeeding Thunderbolt.

Above: Gliding high above Lake Kennywood, the Rockets were a fun ride anytime.

Right: The fun ending of the Daffy Klub Walk-thru occurred when patrons were dropped onto this "magic carpet" which delivered them to the exit.

127

"All Kiddieland rides are five cents with six-ticket strips for twenty-five cents. Auto race and miniature train are ten cents. Our Kiddieland requires a large staff of over 30 employees since we handle our kids gently, lifting and strapping many of them into cars and seats, which takes time.

"Compared with adult rides with less payroll, and speedier operation resulting in greater capacity, Kiddieland is not as profitable, but its value as an attraction and good will and business builder cannot be over estimated.

"Little patrons of Kiddieland rides are going through the Kindergarten of Park patronage and their loyal support remains as they grow up and 'graduate' to the larger flat rides and coasters that are standard installations."

Kennywood added to its Kiddieland a jet kiddie ride in 1948 and a sail boat ride in 1949.

This Kiddieland, which helped build the grown-up patronage, would find a new serious competitor in the 1950's with the advent of television. How Kennywood coped with television is one of the major stories of the 1950's.

For many years the entrance to Kennywood's Kiddieland consisted of children's blocks supporting the letters Kiddieland and some of Disney's seven dwarfs. Note that Kiddieland tickets were still five cents each in 1949.

Ringing the bell and turning the helm were great fun aboard The U.S.S. Idaho, left. This little ship with its sister ships traveling on an undulating track, giving it a wave-like sensation. A miniature version of the Tumble Bug themed with turtles was a very popular ride. The youngsters enjoyed slipping and sliding on the turtle's backs as the ride went on its circular and undulating course. (Below)

The Railroad (opposite—bottom) ran in back of Kiddieland, along the bluff overlooking the Monongahela River. Note the small covered coaches had protective bars to keep the young riders inside.

Below: Small water rides proved to be very popular with the youngsters. The Kiddie Old Mill was constructed in the 1930's and the Sailboats were purchased after the war. The Swan Boats added a touch of nautical class to the ride.
Having one of the largest Kiddielands in North America, Kennywood was in a good position to exploit the baby boom following World War II. When some of the original kiddie rides wore out, the Park replaced them with the newest and latest models.

Kennywood had constant trouble with the bottom of its swimming pool, as many small coal mines honeycombed the area under the pool and park. The Park was forced to spend thousands of dollars every year in replacement and/or repair of the pool bottom thanks to subsidence of the terrain. To hold the antiquated filtration system the pool was improved several times during its life.

130

9

The Fifties:
Kennywood Survives TV

The fifties were a time of change. Suits, ties, and dresses gave way to pedal-pushers, bermuda shorts, and short shorts. The Dance Hall and swimming pool closed, although the swimming pool reopened by the end of the decade. Kennywood, the Trolley Park, lost its street car line at the end of the decade, but new traditions were developed as Kennywood moved into the 1950's.

A small twelve-inch bluish-gray picture first appeared in Pittsburgh in 1950. The first television station was WDTV (later its call letters were changed to KDKA), which was soon followed by WQED in 1953, WIIC in 1957 and WTAE in 1958. Many experts said that amusement parks and motion pictures days were numbered. Who would leave home when cowboys and Indians, puppets, music, variety, and old movies were brought into your home free?

(WIIC's call letters were changed in later years to WXPI.)

Below: From the Howdy-Doody Television Show, Clarabell the Clown appeared many times in the Park during the 1950's and 60's. Note in this picture, taken on the Jack Rabbit, the seltzer bottle in Clarabell's hand and the apparently slightly upset wet policeman at the left!

Overleaf: The Lone Ranger, played by Clayton Moore, appeared at Kennywood Park in 1957. His appearance marked the high point of appearances of TV personalities.

Even local TV personalities like the Wilkins EZC Ranch Gals attracted huge throngs of fans. An announcement board at the right of the stage touts the forthcoming appearance of the well-known movie and TV star Gabby Hayes. The Bandshell had been completely refurbished in the 1960's, with the old decorative trim removed and neon tubing added.

Kennywood as early as 1950 had two weekly advertising spots on WDTV. Their early TV ads were on Friday at 6:45 p.m. and Saturday at 7:00 p.m. before the Lone Ranger Show.

By 1951, Kennywood was presenting local TV personalities like Bill Brant of TV Revue and Buzz Aston and Bill Hinds, a local singing duo. In 1953 Abbie Neal and her Ranch Gang and Al Morgan, the virtuoso of the Flying Fingers, appeared in the Music Pavilion.

The first national TV performers, Captain Video and his Video Ranger (Al Hodge and Don Hastings), played Kennywood in 1953.

Members of the Howdy Doody Show appeared regularly from 1953 into the early 1960's. They were led by Clarabell the Clown with some of the following as supporting cast: Princess Summer Fall Winter Spring, Chief Thunder Chicken, Buffalo Vic or Buffalo Eddie, and Zippy the Chimp.

Other local personalities who appeared in the 1950's were Marty Wolfson, Johnny Costa, Ida Mae and Happy, Wilkens E. Z. C. Ranch Gals, Joe Negri Trio, Hank Stohl and Knish, Jose Carey, and Sterling Yates.

Superman and other super-heroes appeared at Kenny-wood Park repeatedly in the 1950's and 1960's. Dennis The Menace (shown here clanging a bell) was able to get additional publicity for the Park when local newspapers and television stations interviewed him as a celebrity.

Below, left: A promotional brochure published in 1954.

National performers who appeared were Mary Hartline, Queen of Super Circus, Gabby Hayes, Lassie, Superman (George Reeves) who played Clark Kent the mild-mannered reporter, Circus Boy, Captain Kangaroo (Bob Keeshan), Cisco Kid, Zorro (Guy Williams), and Pinky Lee.

The biggest TV attraction was the Lone Ranger who appeared on August 27, 1957. Over 45,000 faithful fans flooded Kennywood to see the masked man, Clayton Moore, who played the Lone Ranger. He arrived in an orange Cadillac, but soon left it for his horse Silver. Over 8,000 spectators jammed the music plaza area to get a glimpse of a real live TV star. The following year, Kennywood tried to top this with a doubleheader of the Lone Ranger and Lassie but it didn't draw as big a crowd as the Lone Ranger had alone.

Kennywood wisely used TV personalities to bring people to the Park. They found that people wanted to see, hear, and touch the people who they saw on the little screen in their living room.

In 1955 Brady McSwigan commented, "TV is wonderful for parks, especially aimed at kids, but it is getting awful expensive to use. We have ten spots a week of a minute, twenty and ten second makeup. We are using no radio. Kids don't listen to it any more, do they?"

Kennywood continued its policy of adding new rides through the 1950's. Carl Henninger and Brady McSwigan were always on the outlook for exciting new rides. The most spectacular rides added in the 1950's were the Rotor and Wild Mouse.

In the Rotor, 30 riders lined up around the inside of a twenty-foot cylinder. Then the cylinder revolved and when it got to spinning at sufficient speed, the floor lowered. Instead of slipping down with the floor, the riders were left hanging like human flies against the wall. The centrifugal force overcame the downward pull of gravity. When the rotor slowed down again the floor came up again under the riders' feet.

The Rotor was the first European ride placed in Kennywood. It was brought in on a concession basis by Charles Freeman of London, England, between

134

The Rotor was Kennywood's first imported ride. The Park did not own it, but leased it as a concession with a British firm. It was advertised as "The World's Greatest Sensation" and many people were willing to pay the price of admission merely to watch it. Centrifugal force held the riders against the wall of the rotating cylinder as the floor pulled away from their feet.

1955 to 1958. Every year Freeman would send an employee from England to operate and repair the ride. Kennywood would have the employee enter the Country each year in March.

The Rotor, which had been placed between the Dance Pavilion and Pony Track, was replaced in 1958 by a Wild Mouse. The Wild Mouse was built by B. A. Schiff of Miami, Florida. Its appeal was based on an element of risk. The ride had single roller coaster cars, which were raised up an incline. They then would scoot down and up dips and around tight curves which gave the sensation of flying into space. The little cars seemed to move in mid-air without any visual means of support. The flimsiness of the Wild Mouse structure added to the element of danger.

Two new rides from Eyerly Aircraft of Salem, Oregon, were added during the 1950's. A Roll-O-Plane was purchased in 1950 and an eight-arm Octopus in 1952. The Dipsy Doodle (Flying Scooter) returned in 1954 for a few seasons.

Two Ferris wheels and a Scrambler ride called Crazy Orbit were purchased from Eli Bridge Company of Jacksonville, Illinois, in 1959. A Paratrooper replaced the old Ferris wheel by the merry-go-round. Two Ferris wheels which were run in tandem replaced the Looper near the Music Plaza.

The Old Mill was rethemed to a trip around the world with nine new scenes in 1957. The old Cuddle-

Opposite: Two new rides were purchased from the Eyerly Aircraft Company of Salem, Oregon; the Roll-O-Plane and the 8-Armed Octopus. These rides demonstrate the movement toward more lighting and "flash."

The Wild Mouse was developed in Europe and sold in America, but the Kennywood machine was made in this country by B. A. Schiff. Tiny cars on a narrow track with fast drops and quick curves create a thrilling sensation. The Mouse caused a lot of minor bruises to patrons and the Park decided to remove it after only a few seasons. The ride was a favorite of dating couples as tiny two-seater cars required them to get really close.

Dual Eli Wheels were purchased in 1959 and erected near the Pippin which can be seen in the background of the picture at the left. These two rides were especially effective at night with their enormous circumference of lights spinning in the dark.

Up was removed in 1954 and replaced with a Pretzel dark ride. It was first unnamed, then called the Mystery Ride and later called the Zoomerang after a television contest (on the Happy and Ida Mae Show) to name it.

In 1957 a Roundup was purchased from the Hrubetz Company of Oregon. It would tilt up almost upright while holding the riders by centrifugal force.

Kennywood continued to update its coasters. Management wanted to add additional track to either the Pippin or Jack Rabbit but they weren't able to do this until the 1960's. New streamlined coaster cars were bought from National Amusement Devices for the Pippin in 1958. The new Pippin cars had a revolving headlight, which gave the ride an eerie quality at night. Edwin Vettel, Sr. of West View built new Jack Rabbit trains in 1952 for Kennywood.

Andy Vettel, the Park's engineer and Edwin's nephew, designed and supervised the construction of an additional 440 feet of track for the Little Dipper. This was done so that two trains could be used.

With the continuation of the postwar baby boom, Kennywood made some important changes in its Kiddieland. It continued to update and replace its kiddie rides. A new entrance made of giant toy soldiers was added in 1953. In the same year a circular tiny tot comfort station topped with a huge Mother Goose and decorated with nursery rhymes was built.

A hand car railway with 300 feet of track and a new speedboat ride were added in 1953. A Rodeo was purchased from Norman Bartlet in 1952. It had 12 adult-sized horses with western saddles. The horses went up and down in a galloping action and the riders had a pistol with which they could shoot bandits in the center of the ride. When an electronic hit was scored, bells would ring and lights would flash. A Bulgy the Whale was added the same year to Kiddieland. A new miniature Sky Fighter was purchased in 1950.

Another exciting ride added in the 1950's was the paratrooper (top picture) manufactured by the Hrubetz Company. In this ride, patrons with their feet dangling swing from side to side while going around the inclined circle.

The Little Dipper (or Dipper, for short) is Kennywood's junior coaster. The ride was built in 1947 with additional track added by Andy Vettel in 1951.

(Left) Patrons exiting from the Old Mill in an Old Mill Boat with dragon heads. As new boats had to be purchased from time to time the dragons were removed from the old boats and switched to the new.

Some new attractions at Kennywood in the 1950's included the Round-up (top), Mother Goose changing area, and a new dark ride (right) un-named at the time of this picture but later titled "The Zoomerang." The Zoomerang was themed with an African flavor featuring apes, elephants, lions, etc.

The Little Turnpike ride was added in 1955. It had a 600-foot track, a tunnel, and little caddy cars. When the Whirly Bird helicopters were first purchased from Allan Herschell in 1958, they were placed in the regular Park. Later they were moved into Kiddieland.

The most popular souvenir in the 1950's was cowboy hats. Other big sellers were Hawaiian leis, cedar boxes, 7″ hula dolls, pin wheels, and Japanese straw cooliehats that cost nine cents and were sold for forty cents.

As in every business, some traditions must die. In 1953, both the dance pavilion and swimming pool closed. The dance pavilion that had played some of the most famous bands from Billy May to Rudy Vallee closed in June of 1953. The old Dance Hall was used for the Enchanted Forest walk-thru in 1954 and later converted into a dark ride in 1964.

In 1958, Kennywood put in its own closed circuit TV system as part of the "Enchanted Forest." The camera was set up in a corner of the tilt room to catch the antics of the patrons. The TV receiver was

Kennywood's Ballroom was closed in 1952 and a Children's Walk-Thru—The Enchanted Forest—was placed in the old building. It featured small dioramas such as the one at the left.

U Drive-Em Boats were placed in the Park Swimming Pool after it was closed for swimming in 1953, but the boats were removed after the 1957 season and the pool re-opened for swimming in July of 1958.

set up over the cashier's booth at the entrance to catch passers-by. The novelty of appearing on TV stimulated business in the walk-thru for a few years.

The swimming pool closed to swimming in June of 1953 and was replaced with "U Drive-'Em" Boats for three seasons. The 357 by 180 foot pool reopened to the public on Memorial Day, 1956. A new grassy area was added for sun bathers. In 1958, after the pool was filled with 1,750,000 gallons, it was discovered that the pool was leaking at the rate of 40,000 gallons a day. The pool had to be drained so that the deep end could be repaired. It reopened in July.

Some new traditions were started, such as the construction of an antique wishing well with an old oak bucket in 1953. People started putting coins into the well and Kennywood decided to donate the money to Children's Hospital of Pittsburgh. Park police had to pull twelve children out of the well in its first season.

144

"STORYBOOK-LAND
ON PARADE"
and Tournament of Music

KENNYWOOD PARK

8 Gala Nights
AUG. 26 thru SEPT. 2

BRING THE CHILDREN

The Fall Fantasy and Tournament of Music was developed by Park management to help business in the slack tail end of the season. It generally lasts 8 days and features local high school bands and majorettes in an nightly parade. The Park provides the floats and Park employees participate in a variety of ways. Note the large book (opposite page, top) which earlier in this volume was shown devoted to President Franklin D. Roosevelt.

One of Kennywood's old traditions was revived after a 30-year absence. Fall Fantasy was a revival of the Mardi Gras celebration of the 1920's. The last several weeks of August had always been a slow period so Kennywood held the first annual fall fantasy Alice in Wonderland on Parade in 1950.

It was followed by such diversified parades as Arabian Nights on Parade, Circus on Parade, and Frontier Days on Parade. Fall Fantasy Parades featured tri-state high school bands and the outstanding majorette winners each year.

In 1958 the ponies were unwound at Kennywood. For 60 years the ponies had been going around the track in a counter-clockwise direction but in 1958 they were dispatched in a clockwise manner.

Kennywood pioneered a fish day 'n hot dogs in 1959. For years many religious groups would not eat meat on Friday. Kennywood's Restaurant Manager, Bill Stagg, was one of the first amusement park managers to serve "tunies" made out of tuna fish which looked and tasted like hot dogs.

Circus acts were continued on the Lagoon Stage in the 1950's. Two of Kennywood's acts were a publicity bonanza in 1953. Rasini and his Rocket Car took an unscheduled dive into the park lagoon. The daredevil from Denmark drove his miniature jet-propelled car down a ramp, turned a complete somersault in mid-air, and landed on the edge of his net. It then flipped into the lagoon narrowly missing a rowboat and finished upside down in four feet of water. Tony Sacramento, long-time merry-go-round operator, helped drag the dazed, slightly water-logged rocketman from the lagoon.

The same year Victoria Zacchini (Miss Victory), daughter of Walter Zacchini, hit her net set upon the lagoon stage off balance and dislocated her elbow. All of the Pittsburgh newspapers ran photos and articles on these accidents. In 1959 the Zacchinis appeared in a double cannon act with Miss Victory and Walter Zacchini being shot out of their cannons at the same time.

Fred Henninger, who had been responsible for the business side of the Park from 1906 until shortly before his death, died in 1950. He had brought his three sons into the business and after his death Carl Henninger became vice-president and continued as general manager. Robert F. Henninger was vice-president and refreshment manager and Harry Henninger replaced his father as treasurer of Kennywood.

For a Park that started as a trolley park, it is a traumatic experience when trolley service is discontinued and the tracks are ripped up. 1958 was the last summer for old # 68 street cars. At the time it was talk of modern, more convenient buses, but there had always been something special about Kennywood's open air trolley and street cars.

So Kennywood moved into the 1960's with many doubts of whether traditional amusement parks might go the way of the street car. Disneyland and its imitators seemed to be the wave of the future. Multimillion dollar theme parks were springing up all over.

Each year more old friends in the amusement park business went out of business. Could a traditional park which featured roller coasters, fun houses, thrill rides and a merry-go-round survive in the 1960's?

The Pippin had a fearful reputation. It was best-known for its double dip (top picture) and its unexpected start. The modern headlighted coaster cars were purchased from National Amusement Devices. Note the 10¢ ticket price.

Opposite: #68 run was known as the "Kennywood Run" by thousands of trolley patrons, but changing times dictated the end of service in 1958. (Carnegie Library of Pittsburgh)

It took one picnic ticket if you were under eight years, and two if over eight to ride the Dentzel Carousel. Notice the woman in the foreground with the coolie hat, thousands of which were sold at stands throughout the Park. Hodge cars, a new ride in the 1950's were real muscle-builders as youngsters provided their own motive power. Rear-end collisons were a frequent occurrence, as faster drivers tried to overtake slower ones.

10

Meeting the Challenges of the 1960's

Kennywood's first band-shell burned on April 24, 1961.

Despite the closing of other parks, for Kennywood the 1960's could be called the decade of business as usual. The Park added at least one new ride every year, proving wrong those who said Kennywood could not survive. The dark ride, railroad, and walk-thru were rethemed and other improvements were made. A calm surface prevailed at Kennywood, but there were strong new currents running in the amusement park industry. Family-owned parks like Euclid Beach near Cleveland, Chicago's Riverview, and Forest Park in St. Louis closed for good. Rides were more expensive every year. New rides like log flumes and miniature gasoline cars were being developed. Single price admission was replacing tickets in the large theme parks. How Kennywood adjusted to these new currents is the real story of the 1960's.

In 1960, the Pennsylvania Railroad decided to drop all short excursion business and cut off 22 picnic trains to Kennywood Park. The auto started to cast its spell over the picnic train when the price of cars got within the reach of ordinary families, but oldsters still liked to talk about the fun of picnic trains.

Carl O. Hughes was named Kennywood's manager in 1960. He had started as summertime publicity director for the Park in 1947 while still working as a sports writer for the *Pittsburgh Press*. He had become a full-time employee in 1956 and was named assistant manager.

1960 saw several old favorites being refurbished, including a new facade on the Racer and a new front on Laff in the Dark. The bridge over the lake was given a futuristic appearance. All of these were designed by John C. Ray of California.

The Bubble Bounce was modernized with clown faces by Allan Hawes Company and was renamed the Bouncer.

Enchanted Forest walk-thru in the old dance pavilion was changed to Enchanted Castle, with towers and spirals on another new front. The interior was redone with a spine-tingling new dungeon.

Next to the Enchanted Castle in Kiddieland was a Kiddie Carousel from Germany with motorcycles, fire engines, racing cars, and even a miniature street car.

The tradition of accepting leftover picnic tickets at the end of the season continued, with 8 bikes (4 boys and 4 girls) being given away.

The Wild Mouse was removed after the 1960 season and was replaced by a European import, the Calypso. It was the first high flash ride, with over 5,208 lights illuminating it.

Laff-In-The-Dark received its last new front in the early 60's. John C. Ray, a well-known Park Designer, did the new facade.

The old Dance Pavilion that had been turned into The Enchanted Forest walk-thru became the Enchanted Castle in the early 1960's. The doodad-ed bridge across Lake Kennywood was another John Ray design masterpiece.

151

The Zoomerang dark ride near the Pippin became the Safari in 1961. A giant 16-foot high African warrior decorated the front. The ride had man-eating pygmies, huge jungle snakes, and witch doctors jumping out in the most unexpected places at riders. The ride was entered through the jaws of a mammoth ape.

A modern front and larger grassy area were added to the swimming pool. After 35 years of being just Kennywood's swimming pool, it became "Sunlite Pool."

A great tradition came to an end when Kennywood's Bandshell burned on opening day 1961. Fire was discovered about 2 a.m. and Homeville and Duquesne fire companies battled the blaze for about an hour. The fire was visible from Braddock and North Braddock, as flames lit the sky over the Monongahela River.

Eddie Pupa's orchestra, a frequent performer in the Bandshell, had played the first and last concert of the 1961 season on that fateful opening day.

The fire was caused by a short circuit. Although the shell itself was a total loss, the 5,500 seats in front of it were not damaged.

Firemen poured water on the Pippin roller coaster, which was located next to the Bandshell, and it was saved from the flames by their quick action. In retrospect, the saving of the old Pippin coaster was much more important than anyone realized. Part of the Pippin was later used in the Thunderbolt which signaled Kennywood's renaissance.

The Park knew it needed a new bandstand and it started design and construction of a new one immediately. On Memorial Day, 1962, Kennwood dedicated its new bandstand with Al Morgan, music star of TV and radio. Also appearing at the opening was Baron Elliot and his Stardust Melodies. The new bandstand was made in a hyberbolic shape with its sweeping roof balancing on two contact points on the stage. The old bandstand had been made of wood and plaster, but the new one was steel and concrete.

Brady McSwigan was always deathly afraid of fire; he usually put the park to bed each night. However, on opening night of 1961 an electrical short circuit initiated the fire which destroyed the bandshell which was built in 1900. Note in the photo (opposite page, lower), the superstructure of the Pippin which was saved by the prompt action of the fire department. Top, left: Firemen continue to wet down the smouldering ruins. The grand opening of the Starvue Plaza took place the following season.

Also, in 1961, Kennywood produced a 20-minute historic film called "The River That Remembered." The film was provided free of charge to school groups and organizations. It was produced by Pittsburgher William G. Beal and narrated by KDKA's Ed Schaughency.

For the small fry, a flying saucer ride from the San Antonio Roller Works was added. Kids could control their own flying saucers as they swirled and dipped on this circular ride.

The major new ride for the 1962 season was the Flying Coaster built by Aeroaffiliates of Fort Worth, Texas. This was another ride designed by Norman Bartlett. Kennywood themed this ride the Kangaroo and added kangaroos around the edges. The ride was a circular device with two-passenger cars which climbed a slope and then fell into space as from a cliff.

Midway through the season, the Dipsy Doodle Flying Scooters' transmission broke down. It was removed and replaced with 12 flying cages which Kennywood called Alle Oop. These only remained two seasons because there were many minor bumps and bruises as the riders tried to get the cage over the top.

During the 1960's, Kennywood presented some top-name musical performers. Some of the record stars who appeared on the Star Vue Stage were Frankie Avalon, Neil Sedaka, Bobby Rydell, Bobby Vinton, and Dion. Perennials who appeared included the Lone Ranger, Lassie, Howdy Doody's Pals, Yogi Bear and Huckleberry Hound, Fred Flintstone, Al Morgan, and Frankie Yankovich.

In 1963, thirty Russians visited Kennywood, mostly riding the Pippin and photographing everything in sight.

Andrew Brady McSwigan, president of Kennywood for 41 years, died October 31, 1964, after a long illness. Kennywood Park under his direction had a period of great expansion in the 1920's. His pioneer amusement park architecture that combined showmanship and design survived the Depression and World War II.

The year after Brady McSwigan died Kennywood Boulevard in front of the Park was finally completed. Construction had started in 1962 on the 1.55-mile

Kennywood entered the space age when they purchased a little Flying Saucer ride for Kiddieland in the 1960's. For those youngsters with their feet on the ground, the Park bought a ride from Germany which featured little automobiles, motorcycles, and even a little European-styled trolley car.

Bottom: The Stark Bubble Bounce was re-styled with new cars and clown heads and re-named the "Bouncer."

stretch of the highway which ran from Rankin Bridge to the Kennywood Bridge. Traffic was detoured over and around it to the Park. Due to construction delays, the road didn't formally open until May 2, 1965.

Spaceships were added in Kiddieland, the Choo Choo Railroad was rechristened Ol Mon River Railroad, and a long tunnel was added.

The Gunsmoke Shooting Gallery was added along the lake between the Jack Rabbit Coaster and Pastime Building. Oldtimers remember the Pastime Building as the Daffy Klub.

In 1965, Carl Henninger became president of Kennywood. Even though Kennywood didn't own the land the park was built on and operated on a short-term lease, Henninger wanted Kennywood to build some major attractions to keep up with the competition. This he did by the end of the decade.

With the completion of Kennywood Boulevard, Kennywood built a new entrance. It was constructed of columns of Belgian block—old Pittsburgh Street cobblestones.

The Dipsy Doodle received a new set of gears and a paint job and became the Flyer. At the end of the season, Kennywood sold its Octopus and Schiff cages.

Kennywood in the late 1960's and 1970's offered country and western stars in the month of May. Some of the stars included Lester Flatt and Earl Scruggs, Grandpa Jones, Hank Snow, Ferlin Husky, Tex Ritter, and Roy Acuff.

The Turnpike replaced Laff in the Dark near the main entrance in 1966. It was the most expensive ride built in Kennywood since the major roller coasters of the 1920's. Costing over $100,000, the Turnpike is a scaled-down parkway with 22 two-passenger gasoline engine sports cars. The road is about half a mile long and has two bridges and underpasses. The cars were built by Arrow Development Company. The ride was patterned after the Turnpike in Disneyland.

The little seven horsepower cars could travel at a maximum speed of 12 miles per hour. Part of the layout was a miniature Gulf Service Station where the riders got in the cars. The whole Turnpike was a first-class operation with landscaping and beautiful lighting for night driving.

Kennywood had adopted the kangaroo as one of their symbols in the 1960's. Therefore it was logical to theme their new ride, the flying coaster, "The Kangaroo." Center: The little choo-choo railroad's cars were modified in the 1960's with the roofs and grillwork removed. Bottom: Brady McSwigan, president of Kennywood Park from 1923 until his death in 1964 was a leader in the amusement park industry. He served two terms as president of the National Amusement Park Association.

The Park's new ride, The Turnpike, was a major commitment to the future, costing more than $100,000. The ride required extensive permanent improvements. If the Park was forced to close or move these improvements would be lost. Management went all-out to create an excellent ride in spite of the obvious financial risk.

Compare the new streamlined cars on their turnpike with the Mangels "Coney Car", originally installed in the 1920's.

The Zacchinis, long favorites at Kennywood, appeared in a double cannon act in the late 1950's and early 60's. Walter and his daughter Victoria (Miss Victory) were shot from a cannon located on the edge of the lake into their net on the island stage.

Less spectacular acts like the Juggling Jandars appeared on the island stage. For many young Pittsburghers, Kennywood was the only place they were able to see live performances of this nature now that fewer circuses traveled the land.

The Trabant, purchased from Chance Manufacturing Company of Wichita, Kansas, was another new ride in the 1960's.

For the third time in ten years Kennywood re-themed their old Dance Pavilion. The Park purchased a Dark Ride from Freedomland, in New York City. They then created a midwest tornado theme, and fronted the building with store fronts reminiscent of the old west.

Another ride from Chance Manufacturing, The Sky Diver, was re-named the "Pop Over" by Kennywood. (Bottom)

For younger kids, a small circular antique car ride was added to Kiddieland. It featured upholstered seats, windshields, and a "rumble" type back seat with two steering wheels for backseat drivers.

A kiddie ride added for two seasons was Shela the Indian Elephant. The attendant who had been hired to help children on and off the elephant went to Kennywood's office early in the afternoon of his first day and asked for a transfer. He complained that the elephant had eaten his lunch, bag and all.

In the middle 1960's, the Gateway Clipper offered a cruise from its main dock in Pittsburgh up the Monongahela to a dock at McKeesport. Bus service was provided to Kennywood and back to Pittsburgh.

The second major ride added in 1966 was a Trabant. This ride's motion resembles a dime spinning on end just before it falls.

1966 was the last year for Mary's Garden. In 1967 it was replaced by an oriental-type garden with fountains.

A cameo scene of General Braddock's ill-fated 1755 encounter with the French and Indians was added to the Mon River Railroad. This scene was created by Special Effects Inc.

The Tornado ride was removed from the Dance Pavilion and replaced with the Ghost Ship dark ride. This new ride took the rider through the hull of an abandoned ship wrecked on the high seas. One of the rooms seemed to rock and there was even a real waterfall. The front designed by Bill Tracey of Amusement Display Associates Inc. of Cape May Court House, New Jersey, had a ghost ship and grinning skeleton to greet passengers. Bill Tracey was one of the great fun house and dark ride designers in the United States. In the 1960's and early 1970's he designed several of Kennywood's fun houses.

158

On occasion the management re-opened the entire Park for Nuns from the Diocese of Pittsburgh. Note the expressions of excitement as the passengers start down a hill on the Pippin.

Upper Right: Ecclesiastical habits were not designed for the rigors of a fast ride like the Kangaroo!

Below: Note the worried nun in the boat holding on for dear life while her sisters paddle away with obvious glee.

The Skydiver Ride was purchased from Chance Manufacturing Company. Kennywood called its ride the Pop Over. The ride was a large wheel standing 75 feet high and carrying two persons. A steering device in the car enabled the rider to turn around in circles, while the wheel structure operated in the manner of a Ferris wheel. As the big wheel turned, gravity made the car "pop" upside down. This ride was very much a teenager ride.

In the middle 1960's, Kennywood hired 450 employees, with about half of them being high school or college students. Carl Hughes quipped in 1967 that, "We've all been having trouble finding personnel. Our policy is to hire anyone who's breathing and warm, and if he says 'thank you' he becomes a manager."

During the winter of 1967–1968, almost unnoticed, one of the most important events in the history of Kennywood Park took place. For years, Carl Henninger had wanted to rebuild either the Jack Rabbit or the Pippin. In 1967, mechanical superintendent Andy Vettel was given the green light to completely rebuild the Pippin. It was decided to move the Whip and its building from a spot next to the Pippin to a new location near the Pony Track and Racer. This created enough room to build a high superstructure with four new hills. Andy Vettel commented, "I laid the new coaster out with the maximum drop and curves that the four-seat coaster cars could negotiate in the space available."

It was decided to place the Trabant inside the new circular section of the coaster. Vettel retained the ravine section of the Pippin with its four devastating drops. The coaster would leave the new structure, dip back into the ravine, up the hill, and negotiate the old flat Pippin turn, which would throw riders to the outside of the coaster car. The coaster then would plunge 90 feet into the ravine before hitting a curved brake run.

The new Thunderbolt roller coaster opened in 1968.

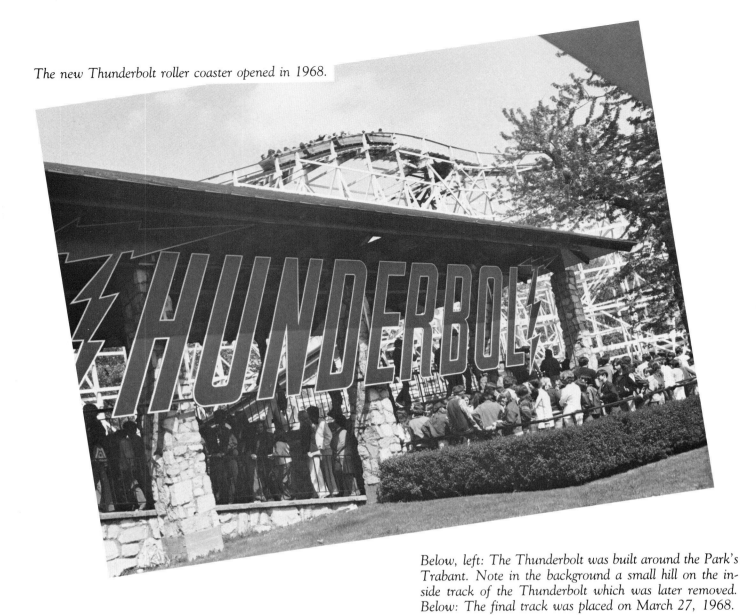

Below, left: The Thunderbolt was built around the Park's Trabant. Note in the background a small hill on the inside track of the Thunderbolt which was later removed. Below: The final track was placed on March 27, 1968.

A contest was held by WTAE television to name the new coaster and the name Thunderbolt was chosen. Kennywood had built a major wooden roller coaster and spent over $200,000 when many amusement park "experts" said roller coasters were dead. Roller coasters were far from dead and in the roller coaster revival of the 1970's, the Thunderbolt was "discovered" and named the Number One roller coaster in the world.

Also, in 1968, the Cuddle-Up built by Philadelphia Toboggan Company returned to Kennywood after an absence of over 30 years. It was placed in a section of the old dance pavilion. Kennywood did what it often did, calling its new Cuddle-Up the Road Runner. Kennywood's earlier Cuddle-Up had been called the Snapper.

Another old favorite returned to Kennywood in 1969 when the Park bought a Caterpillar. The previous Caterpillar purchased in 1923 had been sold in 1945. This Caterpillar was placed near the Penny Arcade in the same location as the original Caterpillar, and has a huge bug cover with a striped canvas top and a blower underneath for extra thrills.

Noah's Ark was completely renovated for the 1969 season. Everything was removed but the wooden ship. New animals, scenes, and stunts were placed in the ship. There was a new entrance through a huge whale with a life-like tongue. This then led to a new mountain with a jungle and tilt room. Patrons now entered the ship from the left rather than the right.

For the small fry Kennywood offered a new Kangaroo ride. Youngsters would sit in big pink pouches which would rise or fall as the rider pushed or pulled on a bar. The Kangaroos were designed by Pittsburgh artist Ivo Zini.

At the end of the 1969 season, the Rock-O-Plane and one of the Ferris wheels were sold.

The popular dress in 1969 was shorts, seersucker blouses, and bell bottom trousers. A rumor circulated that Kennywood wouldn't permit bell bottoms, but park publicity director Ann Hughes issued a statement to the media that bell bottoms were permitted. She did advise mothers with younger children to have them wear red shirts so they could be spotted in a crowd.

The Floral Clock was developed by Kennywood in the 1950's. The floral design is changed regularly. In this picture from the 1960's a giant K for Kennywood is seen. Note the dual Eli wheels in the background.

In 1969 Kennywood celebrated the 20th Anniversary of Fall Fantasy with a parade called "The Best of the Past."

Some of the floats brought back for the Anniversary parade included the real ice skating rink from "Winter Wonderland" in 1966, the stage coach complete with an Indian ambush from "Wild West" in 1955, Red Riding Hood from "Toyland" 1962, The Cow Jumped Over the Moon from "Space Age" 1963, the Magic Mirror from "Alice in Wonderland" 1950, and, of course, Santa Claus from "Holidays" 1960. Each year had some representation. Seven different high school bands walked through the midway each night. In all, seventy bands came to the Park, some from as far as 150 miles away.

Probably nothing illustrates massive changes in the amusement park industry more than Kennywood's first Pay-One-Price Day. For years tickets were king at Kennywood, with school picnic tickets until July 1 and regular tickets thereafter. However, pay-one-price was being adopted by many large regional parks. Finally, Kennywood tried a P.O.P. period August 27, 28, 29, and 30, 1969. The cost was purposely set high ($4.50 per person). It was advertised in the media as "Never before at Kennywood. Every ride in the East's largest amusement park except the ponies and row boats. As many times as you want to ride—noon to 10 p.m." This first P.O.P. period wasn't too successful, but Kennywood was willing to experiment. It didn't discard the old ticket system, but in the seventies it would blend P.O.P. days in and around ticket days.

In 1966 a Pittsburgh columnist printed, "There's a rumor circulating in Pittsburgh show business circles that Kennywood Park may shut down permanently after the current season." There wasn't any truth to this rumor, but it was hard for the Kennywood management to make changes that needed to be made when the park had to do business on a five-year lease. Carl Henninger's decision to build the Turnpike and Thunderbolt on Kennywood's short-term lease were major gambles. If the lease wouldn't be renewed, hundreds of thousands of dollars would have been lost.

For over 60 years, the Kenny heirs had turned down every request by the McSwigans and Henningers to purchase the land on which Kennywood was located. In the 1970's Kennywood would have to spend millions of dollars to keep their park competitive with the large regional parks and they could only do this if they owned the land. Kennywood had to purchase the land the park was built on. The sooner this happened the better.

Zoomerang was re-themed the "Safari" in the late 1960's. It featured a huge African warrior on the facade. In the foreground of the top picture is the Dipsy Doodle, also known as the "Flyer," which over the years had required expensive maintenance and was therefore in and out of service from time to time.

Another old favorite, the caterpillar, returned to Kennywood Park after an absence of 20 years. The new caterpillar was placed in the same position that the old caterpillar had occupied years before.

Kennywood felt that it was time to refurbish Noah's Ark after 23 years of service. Mount Ararat was completely removed, as can be seen, and a new mountain built. Fun-seekers now entered Noah's Ark through a large blue whale with a spongy pink tongue for a floor. New animals on small dollies were lifted into place by a large crane.

Nationality days seemed to thrive in the late 1970's as ethnic groups worked to preserve their identities following the popularity of the book "Roots." In 1976 9 nationality days were held, as indicated on Kennywood's famous outdoor book.

Above: Concessionaire Jimmie Conklin brought in the Bayern Kurve, a ride which suggests a bobsled run in the Bavarian Alps, to Kennywood in the early 1970's. The ride proved so popular that the park bought it.

Below, left: Howdy Doody and Henry (of comic strip fame) were used to gauge the height of youngsters before they were permitted on adult rides.

165

The fourth and final theming of the Old Dance Pavilion took place in 1967. A ghost ship theme was used, with pirates, skeletons, sea creatures, old wrecks, and similar items to scare the patrons. This was the most popular theme that Kennywood ever used in this building.

166

11

Kennywood's Greatest Expansion

In the 1970's Kennywood became known as the Home of the Ultimate Roller Coaster—The Thunderbolt. The greatest expansion in the Park's history took place during this decade and the park was finally able to buy the land on which the Park was built.

Some traditions ended. The Dance Pavilion-dark ride was completely destroyed in a $400,000 fire in 1975. Other traditions like the Scottish picnic and Sunlite Pool came to an end in the decade.

February 26, 1971, was a day of celebration for the Kennywood family as they finally bought from the Kenny heirs the 140 acres on which the Park was located.

The purchase price was $1,300,000. The Kenny family had always been good landlords but major changes which had to be made to compete with major regional theme parks couldn't be made until Kennywood owned the land.

One such improvement was the million-dollar-plus Log Jammer built in 1975. This major log flume was designed and built by Arrow Development Company. It took 10 months to construct the 1,650-foot-long water ride. The channel holds over 90,000 gallons of water, with an additional 500,000 gallons in a storage lagoon. The ride features a 53-foot drop, two lifts, a 27-foot spillway, and over 11 miles of wiring. The flume has a capacity of 1,400 per hour.

The year the Log Jammer opened, an old Kennywood landmark, the Dance Pavilion which had been converted into a dark ride, was destroyed by a fire. The blaze, which occurred June 19, 1975, erupted around 12:15 p.m. It took more than an hour for fire companies from West Mifflin, Munhall, White Oak, and Duquesne plus the park's 15-man force to put out the fire.

Carl Hughes, general manager of the Park, credited the fast action of the fire personnel with preventing the blaze from going out of control. The park's small fire department was the first to put water on the fire.

The fire destroyed two amusement rides, the Ghost Ship, Dark Ride and the Road Runner (Cuddle-Up), which were housed in 5,000 square feet, and two kiddie rides, the Miniature Whip and German Carousel which were located in the rear of the building.

Partially damaged were the Satellite (Round-Up) and the Calypso. The heat was so intense that it melted the superstructure of the Round-Up. Several youngsters inside the Ghost Ship were led to safety by an attendant who then spread the alarm.

Concession stands about 50 feet from the fire were evacuated when the heat began melting the signs. One of the attendants said, "It was just unreal, the fire was hotter than hell."

Kennywood's first million-dollar ride was a log flume "The Log Jammer." This ride was built by Arrow Development Company of Mountain View, California. The ride proved to be an instant success. In the years following its opening its ridership has remained extremely high. The flume has two lifts and two down chutes.

In the best tradition of amusement parks the burning area was roped off, but the rest of the park and other rides and amusements continued in operation. Many visitors boarded high flying rides to watch the blaze from a high vantage point.

Mt. Lebanon and Keystone Oaks school districts were having their annual picnics the day of the fire. Over 2,000 students crowded around the edge of the lake to get a look at the blaze.

Park sweeperettes served donuts, soft drinks, and ice water to firemen and occasionally dumped pitchers of water on the heads of young male employees pressed into service as hosemen. No one was injured but two firemen were overcome by smoke.

The Park's miniature lake, normally dotted with row boats, was cleared as firemen pumped water from it to douse the flames.

Only a few charred beams of the high-ceiling Dance Pavilion (built in 1898) remained after all the flames were subdued about 3 p.m.

Within a few days, the fire damage was cleared and the area sodded. The Calypso was placed back in action within a week.

In 1974 Robert Cartmel, an art professor at the State University of New York at Albany, wrote a feature article called "The Quest for the Ultimate Roller Coaster" for the June 9, 1974, issue of *The New York Times*. After spending years criss-crossing America, he picked Kennywood's Thunderbolt as the Ultimate Roller Coaster.

Cartmel chose the Thunderbolt as number one on his top ten coaster list because its "longer than most" ride time of 1 minute, 58 seconds is filled with a series of long perilous drops, sudden plunges, and bruising turns, all along its 3,300 feet of track. "The Thunderbolt . . . shocks you from the beginning," he said and "while the riders' sighs and giggles of relief can be heard, the train suddenly drops 90 feet before running home. A hill like this at the end of a ride is unthinkable, unfair, but it's just one of the joys to be experienced on this King of Coasters."

Left, above: The Bell Striker gives a young man a chance to show his date how strong he really is. Today more women are willing to take a try at ringing the bell!
Left: A new Grand Prix scooter ride was added in 1977. This ride returned to the two-seat cars of the 1930's.

The Ghost Ship Dark Ride, along with a Cuddle-up, miniature Whip, and German Carousel were destroyed in a spectacular fire caused by an electrical malfunction, on June 19th, 1975, when the Park was in full swing with school picnics. Some patrons stopped to look at the fire while others just continued to ride.

This article signaled the start of the roller coaster revival of the 1970's. Even large theme parks discovered that roller coasters drew patrons by the thousands. In the late 1970's some parks spent as much as 5 or 6 million dollars trying to depose the Thunderbolt, but most experts still considered the Thunderbolt one of the top two or three coasters in the United States.

In 1973, two landmarks disappeared from Kennywood when The Howdy Doody and Henry signs which were used to measure people's height were replaced with Charlie Brown and Snoopy.

One year later, Kennywood adopted a mascot, a costumed character, Kenny the Kangaroo. Kenny's suit weighs 20# and on a 90° day it is like wearing a sauna. The most feared thing for the employee in the kangaroo suit is to have his or her tail pulled. Kenny must stay away from the pony track as the ponies are spooked at the sight of a smiling 6-foot-kangaroo bouncing around.

The Old Mill was rethemed by Ed Hilbert in 1974. It became Hard Headed Harold's Horrendously Humorous Haunted Hideaway. Hilbert designed all the stunts and scenes in Hard Headed Harold's as skeletons set in western scenes.

The merry-go-round wasn't forgotten in the park's rehabilitation. For the bi-centennial year of 1976, the merry-go-round was completely restored. The work was supervised by Henri P. Pohl. First the Dentzel hand-carved animals were stripped to the bare wood, and then art students from Carnegie-Mellon University tenderly refinished the animals, rim, and interior of the 50-year-old merry-go-round. This restoration work was done during the winter, and it looked like the merry-go-round wouldn't be ready for the start of the season. But by working night and day all the horses were done on opening day.

In 1977 the park's Dentzel merry-go-round was registered as an historic landmark by the Pittsburgh History and Landmarks Foundation.

Henri Pohl also rethemed the Ol Mon River Miniature Railroad in 1976, converting it into "Moonshine Valley." The ride featured 40 figures, 23 of them animated. The scenes included a local bath house, covered wagon, blacksmith shop, square

The Monster, by Eyerly Aircraft Company, was another ride brought in as a concession that the Park later decided to buy.

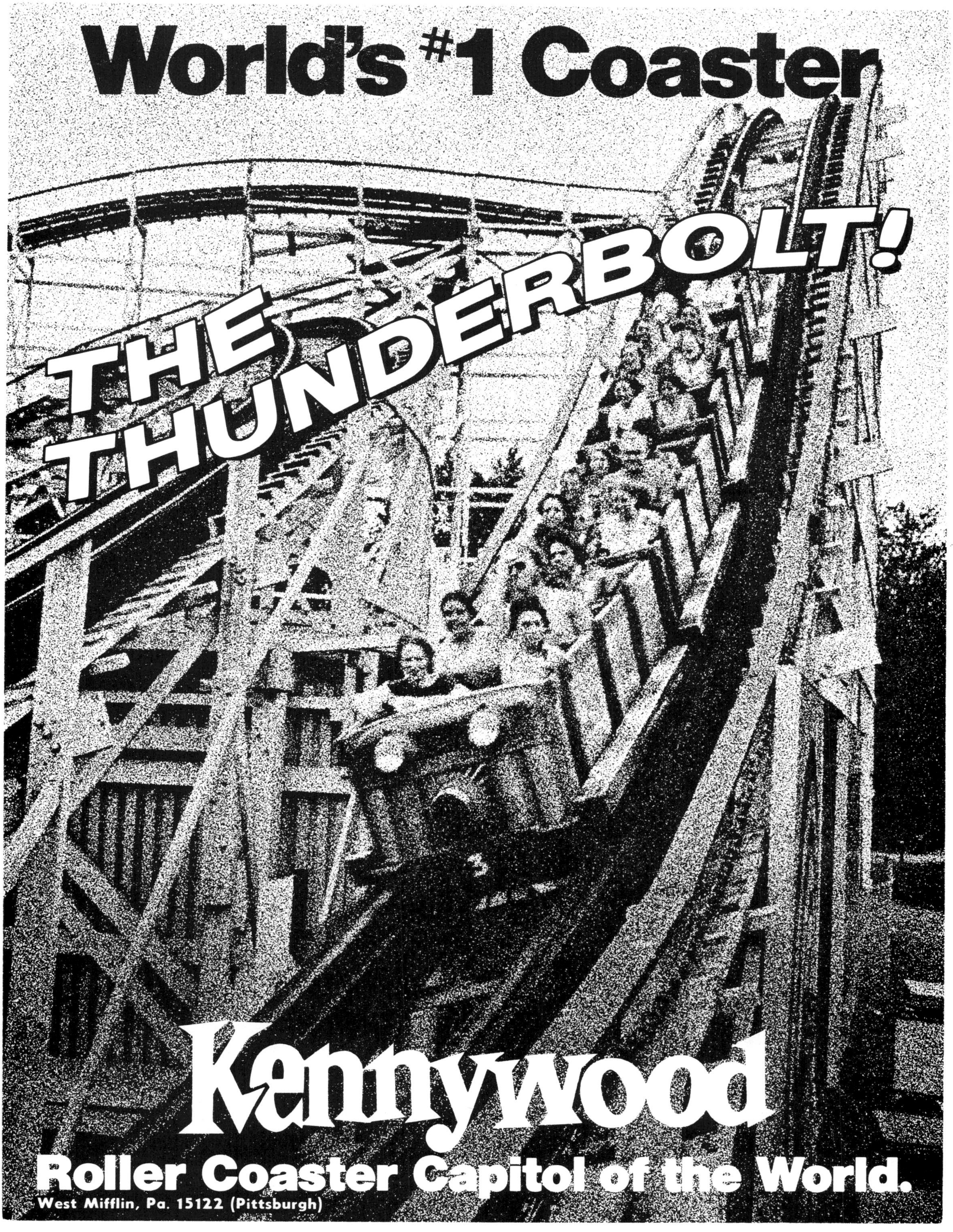
World's #1 Coaster
THE THUNDERBOLT!
Kennywood
Roller Coaster Capitol of the World.
West Mifflin, Pa. 15122 (Pittsburgh)

All of the horses (plus the lion and the tiger) were removed from the carousel the day after Labor Day 1975. A crew supervised by Henry Pohl then removed all of the layers of the old paint and students from Carnegie Mellon repainted the animals. The carousel was completed just in time for opening day in 1976.

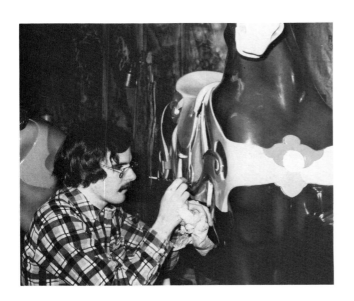

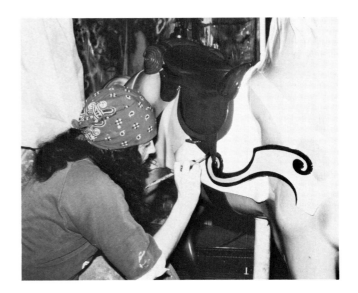

Kennywood's Bi-Centennial "gift" to its patrons was a complete restoration of its 50-year-old Dentzel Carousel. This 4-row carousel is one of the most beautiful machines ever built. It was originally planned for the Sesqui-Centennial Celebration in Phildelphia, but William Dentzel was unable to complete it on time. Kennywood Park then bought it. It features a beautiful Wurlitzer Band Organ.

The carousel sits in the middle of the Park so that riders have a changing panorama of the Park with its lake, rides, gardens, and buildings.

The carousel was repainted with pastel colors. The ceiling was done in a light blue. Gold leaf was widely used on the horses and the rim. This carousel is especially beautiful at night with over 1,500 tiny lights.

dance, and shot-gun wedding. Pohl also did several new scenes for Noah's Ark and LeCachot the same year.

One attraction that didn't survive the 1970's was the Sunlite Swimming Pool. By 1973 maintenance costs were so high the park couldn't afford to operate the pool. During the final season, Kennywood Park had to pump water into the pool for about six hours every night because the floor leaked so badly. The filter system, which had been the most modern system available in the 1920's, was showing its age by the 1970's. The park sadly closed the pool at the end of the 1973 season.

Another much shorter tradition also ended in 1973. Kennywood decided to try and keep its miniature golf course open on weekends at the end of 1973 during September and October. Attendance was so dismal the first two weekends in September it was decided to close early. Thus, this post-season experiment, like roller skating and ice skating before it, ended in failure.

A much older tradition, the Scottish Picnic, ended after 76 years in 1975. With the exception of the Italian Day, most other nationality picnics had shown a steady decline in the 1960's and 1970's. In the aftermath of the TV series "Roots," there was a definite revival of interest in the nationality picnics.

Some of the rides that came in as concessions by Jim Conklin of Canada included the Bayern Kurve, a German manufactured ride which featured famous Olympic bobsleds, a giant German Circle Swing decorated with Old World murals, a Monster from Eyerly Aircraft Company, Salem, Oregon, and a German built Matterhorn.

The Bayern Kurve was so popular that Kennywood bought the ride. Most of the other rides were placed in the park for a season or two and then removed.

Kennywood razed its 39-year-old Rocket Ride in 1979 and replaced it over the lagoon with a new green and yellow Eyerly Monster which was themed the Monongahela Monster. Showing the tremendous inflation in the cost of rides, the Monster Ride cost

A new entrance and fountain was built for Kiddieland in 1976. Note the sign over the entrance "The most beautiful music in the world is children laughing."

178

almost $250,000. Under the platform Kennywood built an entertainment area for live music or just sitting around.

Carl Hughes commented in 1977 that "the theme parks have learned from us and we have learned from them. Theme parks are putting in thrill rides to bring in new customers while traditional parks like Kennywood are putting in live shows and have costumed employees, devices originated by theme parks."

Kenny Kangaroo, Kennywood's first costumed character, was joined by such other characters as Colonel Bimbo Fraudwater and Geeters in 1975.

In 1978 a puppet show by Trotter Brothers was given in Kiddieland. The following season three live shows, the Honeybear Band Show with Goldilocks, Spellbound, a magic show and the Razz Ma Tazz Jazz Band appeared on the new Garden Entertainment Stage under the Monongahela Monster.

Major improvements were made to Kiddieland in the 1970's. After the Dance Pavilion fire a new mall-like entrance was created to Kiddieland. In the middle of the entrance is a fountain which was dedicated to the Kenny family. Old-fashioned lamps and cobblestones from Pittsburgh streets were used to give the new area a turn-of-the-century atmosphere.

Kiddieland rides were added, including a Mini Bouncer and a Honda motorcycle ride, both from the San Antonio Roller Works. A Red Baron Ride was purchased from Chance in 1979. It cost $33,550 which was more than most adult rides cost in the 1960's.

Carl Henninger became chairman of the board of Kennywood in 1975 and was replaced as president of the park by his brother Harry Henninger, Sr. Harry Henninger, Sr. helped negotiate the Kenny land deal and he was the moving force behind the park's decision to build the Log Jammer. When he passed away in 1976, Carl Hughes became president and Harry Henninger, Jr. became general manager of the Park.

Harry Henninger, Jr. was especially interested in construction and development and with the approval of Carl Henninger and Carl Hughes Kennywood undertook its largest development in 1976.

Perhaps it should be called redevelopment rather than development, because as much of the old park was preserved as possible. Cities could study Kennywood's redevelopment to see how urban renewal should be run.

The old Dance Pavilion area was heavily landscaped with spruce, oak, maple, and flowering crab trees. A new Super Round-Up from Hrubetz was placed next to the Calypso. A new games building was also constructed in the area formerly occupied by the dance pavilion. The games building was converted into a pizza and spaghetti restaurant in 1980.

Trotter Bros. brought their puppet show to Kennywood in 1978, to the delight of all the kiddies, and even some of the adults. Jeeters (center) clowns with author's daughter.

Kennywood brought back live acts (vaudeville) in 1978 when they built a new garden entertainment stage along the edge of the lake. Acts vary on this new island stage from magic shows to costume shows to rock musical groups.

A new auto-scooter ride was built next to Kennywood Boulevard in 1977. This building, like others built after 1971, was much more substantial than earlier ones for the Park now owned the land on which they stood.

Lake Kennywood became smaller when a new retaining wall was built along the edge near the Racer where the dance pavilion had been. This new area was used for buffer planting and cobblestone walkways around the southern section of the lake. The island in the lagoon was replaced with a new stage which had dressing rooms built underneath.

Kennywood started to develop a completely new ride and service area behind the office and Noah's Ark, in part of the pay parking lot in 1977. The miniature golf course was relocated and a winding walkway led from the pedestrian tunnel to the new area located behind the park office.

A new 14-car Cuddle-Up was purchased to replace the Cuddle-Up lost in the dance pavilion fire. It was enclosed in a 38-foot high bright orange membrane tent like structure from Helios Tension Products of Japan.

The Loop-O-Plane and Roll-O-Plane were moved from near the miniature golf course to a spot behind the park office. The Ferris wheel was also moved into the new area.

The old service building located between the office and Noah's Ark was razed and its restrooms were rebuilt for 1978.

A new 1,600-foot general service building along with a skee ball-arcade building (Playdium) were constructed in the new area behind the office.

A $350,000 16-car Enterprise from Huss of West Germany was planned for this new area for 1977. The park couldn't get the ride delivered in time so the ride didn't make its debut until 1978.

Forty new Reverchon scooter cars were purchased in 1977 for the Grand Prix.

A 60-foot dome theater building was added to the area in front of Noah's Ark. It was used as a Cinesphere Theater which showed film on a 65-foot diameter screen. The 29-foot high geodesic dome was made of cloth supported from the outside by a network of aluminum bars.

In 1978 the park's office building was renovated. A group sales area was added next to the office.

Robert F. Henninger, who was a vice-president of the park and head of the Kennywood Refreshment Company, died in 1972. When he took over the Refreshment Company in 1946, it consisted of the Casino restaurant and a handful of snack stands. In 26 years, many snack stands were added and the volume of business more than doubled. There was some talk about removing the Casino but Robert Henninger encouraged the park to keep it. It was remodeled in 1971 restoring the historic beauty with its high tin ceiling, exposed wood beams, and slow-moving ceiling fans.

Robert Henninger was replaced at the Refreshment Company by his son, F. W. Henninger.

Another new area has been developed in back of the Kennywood Office. This area contained, in the 1970's, a Tilt-A-Whirl, an Enterprise from West Germany, a Roll-O-Plane and a Loop-O-Plane, a Cuddle-up, and a number 16 Eli Wheel. The new area also contained a service building, a small arcade, and new rest rooms.

Left: The Monkey Water Game is just one of the many new games brought to the Park in the recent period. The restaurant was extensively remodeled in the early 1970's, and a patio dining area covered with yellow and white striped fabric was added. Good french fries have long been a Kennywood hallmark, and a new all-potato refreshment stand was built.

Above: Another annual floral display is the American Flag, which is planted in late May.

Kennywood was extremely fortunate to have members of the younger generation ready, willing, and able to fill important positions in the park. Many other successful amusement parks, including West View, had decided to close when the founders passed away and no one in ownership was interested in management.

Carl Henninger encouraged Harry Henninger, Jr. and F. W. Henninger to take over important positions in Kennywood when the two grandsons of F. W. Henninger were still in their twenties.

As Kennywood grew and became bigger, it had developed quality management from both inside and outside the family. As Kennywood looked forward to the 1980's it had a tight, well-organized staff of full-time employees heading up games, food, rides, picnic booking, maintenance, security, planning, and development.

Two major changes occurred in Lake Kennywood in the 1970's. In the picture above, the Rockets were removed. (Replaced by a Monster Ride). Part of the lake was filled in and the Garden Entertainment Stage was built underneath. The picture below shows the construction of a new island stage in 1975. The lake was drained to make construction easier.

In 1979 the Auto Race, also known as the Auto Ride, celebrated its 50th Anniversary. The cars have undergone extensive modification over the years, but the track layout remains the same. Notice the striped employee uniforms which are now the official uniforms of Kennywood Park. The famous Kennywood yellow signs can sometimes be seen up to 100 miles away from the Park.

12

Looping into the 1980's

The Laser Loop—what a way to start the 1980's! A shuttle loop 139 feet high and a 72-foot vertical loop are featured on Kennywood's new ride for 1980. The Laser Loop was built by Anton Schwarzkopf of West Germany and marketed by Intamin A.G. of Switzerland. The Park's second million-dollar ride was designed by Reinhold Spieldiener, a Swiss engineer.

The Laser Loop starts from a loading station located along a straight section of track. The train, similar to those on a roller coaster, is catapulted by a large fly-wheel and coupling mechanism in less than 5 seconds to a speed of 54 mph.

After bursting out of the station, the train whips through the vertical loop, which is 46 feet in diameter. Hardly is that sensation finished when it climbs an incline 139 feet at an angle of 70°. As the train reaches this highest point, riders experience about 34 percent G's, which is near weightlessness.

Here the car stalls out, the passengers looking at nothing but blue sky ahead. There is nowhere to go but backwards, so backwards it goes!

As the train falls backwards, this G force remains constant, such that if a rider chooses to keep his eyes closed, he would be unaware that he was falling backwards.

The train reverses through the loop and up a second incline of 111 feet, also at a 70° angle. Riders get the impression of being totally vertical, looking straight down. Again the car stalls out, then plummets back to the station.

The Laser Loop required moving the Park entrance from the pay parking lot. The new pedestrian entrance was built directly under the 72-foot high loop.

The Skooter building was razed to make way for this new pedestrian entrance in September 1979. The 70-year-old Skooter building was first used as a fun house under such names as Hilarity Hall, King Tut's Tomb, and the Bug House. It was converted to Skooters in 1935. For 45 years millions of patrons waited for the sound of the metal gong to let them know when their little scooter cars would come to life.

The Pony Track, which had occupied part of the

Overleaf: Kennywood's second million dollar ride was the Laser Loop, opened in 1980. It is a shuttle loop, manufactured by Anton Schwarzkopf of West Germany. Below: Construction of the Laser Loop took place in the winter of 1979–80 when temperatures at times dropped to 5° above zero.

Andy Vettle, the designer of the Thunderbolt, supervised the construction for the Park. The ride's top speed is 54 miles per hour, just before it hits the loop.

old swimming pool area after it was moved to make room for the Log Jammer, was moved again to a location in, under, and around the 139-foot end of the Laser Loop. The ponies, who seemed to be able to adjust to anything, didn't seem to mind the catapulting train.

A new midway was constructed behind Noah's Ark to connect the Enterprise and Cuddle-Up area with the new entrance. Along this new midway was the access to the Laser Loop launching station, a pond with radio-operated miniature boats, and the old swimming pool refreshment stand. This stand was remodeled into a game with life-sized plush animals, and a new refreshment outlet featuring fresh fruits and fresh-squeezed juices.

Bill Henninger, general manager of the Kennywood Refreshment Company, attempted an all you could get on a tray promotion in the Casino Cafeteria for $4.50. Unfortunately, Pittsburghers know how to load a tray and Bill was forced to drop the promotion after the first two weekends in May. About 300 of the park's 1,000 employees worked in food and beverages.

Kennywood has a happy "family" of employees. Generally, 40 to 50 percent of the park employees return every year, which makes training at the beginning of the season easier.

The Magic Show, Wizard of Oz, and Razz Ma Tazz returned to the Garden Stage under the Monongahela Monster.

One of the highlights of the 1980 season was a convention of the American Coaster Enthusiasts. Almost 300 coaster fanatics descended on Kennywood to ride the five great coasters. It was an instant love affair with the coaster enthusiasts loving Kennywood and Kennywood loving a group of people who never get their fill of roller coasters.

Associated Press, local newspapers, and TV stations did stories on Kennywood and ACE.

Kennywood's slogan for the 1980's is "Clean and Green." Ray Waugaman, grounds superintendent, is in charge of the grounds. This veteran also oversees the pony track. He combines his two jobs by using a lot of pony manure in the flower beds, and boards the ponies on his Worthington, Pennsylvania, farm in the winter.

The Midway in front of the Auto Ride and Hoot-n' Holler Railroad shows a typical park crowd of fewer children, more senior citizens, and shorter shorts.

Left, above: The Sportsland Building. Left: Kennywood replaced its old faithful aluminum boats with new fiberglass paddle boats in 1981. Above: Kenny the Kangaroo is now Kennywood's official mascot. He has even been known to make appearances outside the park during the winter!

Part of the clean and green is over 50,000 perennials used to create such Kennywood specialties as the clocks, flower baskets, kangaroo, and daily calender. There are over 60 hanging baskets spread out around the park. During the off-season these baskets are moved to greenhouses. Kennywood's famous living clock contains over 7,200 plants. The design on the face has been changed a number of times since it was first planted in 1953.

There are more than 5,000 trees in the Park. Hundreds of red oaks, maples, spruce, and flowering crabs have been planted in the last 10 years.

Inflation and million-dollar rides have forced Kennywood to raise general admission tickets to $1.50, senior citizens $.75, and under four years old free. One-price days are $8.

More strolling costume characters have been added: Kenny Kangaroo, Colonel Fraudwater and Geeters have been joined by Yellow Bird and Purple Monster. All of these characters are also used in the Fall Fantasy parades.

In 1979, the Sportsland Building, home to seven different games, was rebuilt. A second floor was added and in 1981 a new dark ride called the Goldrusher was unveiled. The interior scenes for this ride were designed by Maurice Ayers who won an academy award for special effects in the "Ten Commandments." The cars were built by Bradley and Kaye.

The Goldrusher replaced the Ghost Ship, which burned in 1975. Harry Henninger said, "The park likes to have two dark rides because they are high-capacity, family-oriented rides. Since they are covered rides, they are good rides to have on rainy days."

What is Kennywood's future? Harry Henninger, general manager of the park and the person most responsible for development, says, "The park must know its place. Kennywood has always been a picnic park. It started as a Pittsburgh park but over the years it has grown into a regional Western Pennsylvania, Northern West Virginia and Eastern Ohio Park. Our transient trade is limited."

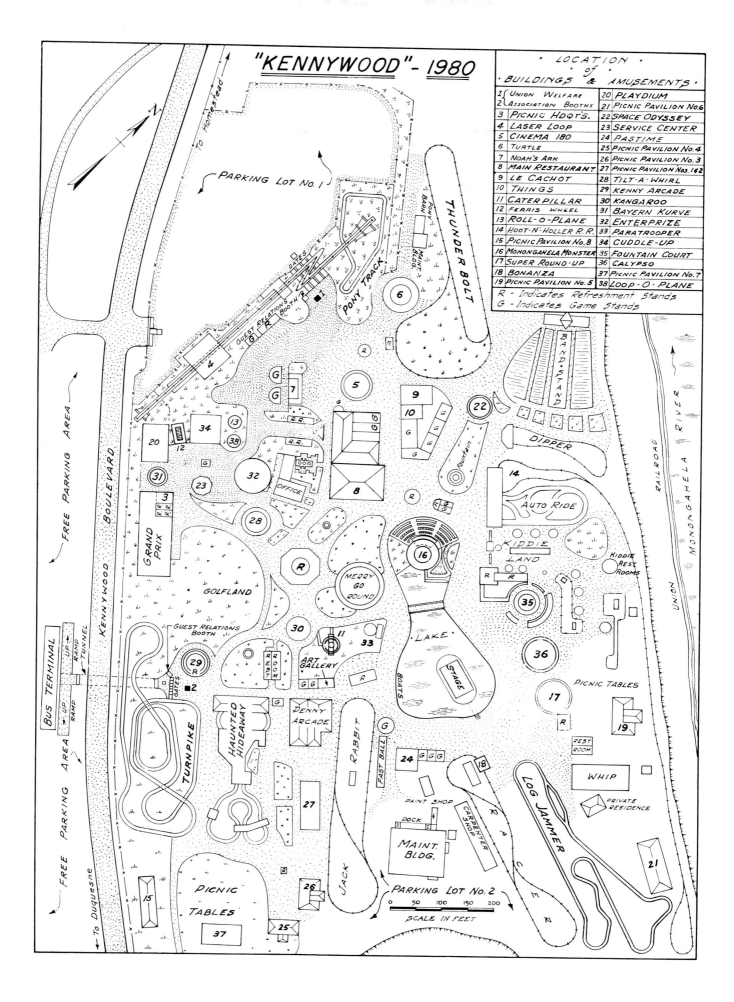

"KENNYWOOD" - 1980

N

PARKING LOT No. 1

THUNDER BOLT

PONY TRACK

TO HOMESTEAD

GATES

GUEST RELATIONS BOOTH

PONY BARN

MAINT. BLDG.

BAND STAND

DIPPER

FREE PARKING AREA

KENNYWOOD BOULEVARD

BUS TERMINAL

TO DUQUESNE

FREE PARKING AREA

RAMP TUNNEL

GATES

GRAND PRIX

GOLFLAND

GUEST RELATIONS BOOTH

REST ROOM

TURNPIKE

HAUNTED HIDEAWAY

DENNY ARCADE

ART GALLERY

MERRY GO ROUND

JACK RABBIT

FAST BALL

PAINT SHOP

DOCK

CARPENTER SHOP

MAINT. BLDG.

PARKING LOT No. 2

OFFICE

AUTO RIDE

KIDDIE LAND

KIDDIE REST ROOMS

FOUNTAIN

LAKE

BOATS

STAGE

PICNIC TABLES

REST ROOM

WHIP

PRIVATE RESIDENCE

LOG JAMMER

RAILROAD

MONONGAHELA RIVER

UNION

PICNIC TABLES

SCALE IN FEET
0 50 100 150 200

LeCachot Dark Ride was re-themed by Bill Tracey of Stone Harbor, New Jersey. It is a good example of the mixing of an old theme—a castle—with a modern theme of a rock musician and a chopper motorcycle.

194

"We must put in the types of rides and attractions which will attract school, industrial, community and general picnics. As our populations grow older, we must offer more things for them like stage shows and more gentle rides like our new dark ride.

"When we put in a major new ride like the Log Jammer or Laser Loop, we must make sure that they will be accepted by the public. We can't afford like the large theme parks to experiment with new million dollar rides which might flop."

Henninger continued, "We will keep up our program of adding more greenery to the park. We know the importance of tradition and we try and preserve as much of it as possible. Even when changes are made we try and keep them as inconspicuous as possible. When we built the new island stage in 1976, very few people realized that it was all new. This is how we will continue to make improvements, without losing the 'something special' that makes Kennywood the great tradition it was for you, your parents, and grandparents."

Kennywood has survived by carefully balancing change and tradition. Some people would like to see the Park remain *Good Old Kennywood*, but is it the Kennywood of the 1930's, 1950's, or the 1970's?

Kennywood has added or changed, built and rebuilt season by season. This is why the Park is still a successful operation while parks like West View, Euclid Beach, and Luna Park have closed.

The Park has tried to minimize change by constructing the new buildings where old buildings stood. After the 1981 season, park management decided to raze the old Penny Arcade building which had been built in 1913. They built a new arcade building on the same spot. Carl Hughes said, "Most people won't even notice that the arcade is in a new building."

What then, is tradition? If there is a new Penny Arcade, a new games building, a new island stage, and even a new bottom for Noah's Ark, then what is being preserved? The purpose is being preserved. If you asked a Pittsburgher in 1899 what was Kennywood, he or she would say a place to have fun, an amusement park. If you ask someone today, the answer would be the same—a place to have fun, an amusement park. The purpose hasn't changed in 80 years. That is tradition.

The Cuddle-Up was purchased from the Philadelphia Toboggan Company in 1976. The Old Mill is now the Haunted Hideaway. Another attraction at the Park is the Spin Art.

Harry W. Henninger, Jr., vice-president and general manager of Kennywood is in charge of future development of the Park.

Carl O. Hughes, president of Kennywood and past-president of the International Association of Amusement Parks and Attractions.

F. W. Henninger, president and manager of the Kennywood Refreshment Company.

The Gold Rusher is a dark ride whose entrance is located near the Thunderbolt. Its little two-seat mine cars travel past the mine machinery before climbing to the second story which is filled with spiders, skeletons, ghosts, and similar paraphernalia.

197

The old Penny Arcade which was built in 1913 was razed after the 1981 season.

Thunderbolt—the Heart of Kennywood

Carousel—The Soul of Kennywood.

. . . after all, Kennywood is just for fun!

Index